Man's Mark on the Land

*Illustrated
with
photographs,
maps, and
charts*

From the Stone Age to the Age of

MAN'S MARK ON THE LAND

the changing environment

Smog, Sewage, and Tar on Your Feet

by ARTHUR S. GREGOR

CHARLES SCRIBNER'S SONS   New York

*Grateful acknowledgment is made to the following
for permission to reproduce illustrative material:*

The American Museum of Natural History, pp. ii (middle), 3, 4 (top), 8, 9,
10, 16, 21, 22, 27, 40, 51, 58, 59, 67, 80, 89, 97, 104; Army Corps of
Engineers, Jared Miller, 102; Australian News and Information Bureau, 7,
111; British Tourist Authority, 39, 71; Consulate General of India, 14;
Consulate General of the Netherlands, 109; E.P.A. Documerica—Charles
O'Rear, 76, —Marc St. Gill, 93; The Metropolitan Museum of Art, 63;
NASA, courtesy of the United Nations, 91; National Film Board of Canada, 4
(bottom), 73; Union Pacific Railroad, 31; United Nations, ii (bottom), 19, 25
(top), 47, 54, 64, 65, 77, 82, 96, 100; United States Department of
Agriculture, 36, 95, 106; United States Department of the Interior, Bureau
of Reclamation, 25 (bottom), 83, 92, 107; United States Department of the
Interior, National Park Service, ii (top), 1, 45.

Maps, charts, and illustrations by Jean Simpson

1 3 5 7 9 11 13 15 17 19   v/c   20 18 16 14 12 10 8 6 4 2

Printed in the United States of America
Library of Congress Catalog Card Number 73–19367
ISBN 0–684–13740–2

Contents

FOR VALERIE AND MARK

We travel together, passengers on a fragile spaceship, dependent on its vulnerable reserves of air and soil; all committed for our safety to its security and peace; preserved from annihilation only by the care, the work, and the love we give our fragile craft.

—Adlai Stevenson

Fifteen thousand years ago the great glaciers of the Ice Age covered large sections of the earth. Today whatever remains of these great sheets of northern ice is found on the top of high mountains in the Arctic regions of Canada, Europe, Greenland, and Alaska. *The Muir Glacier today at Great Bay National Monument in Alaska.*

THE WILDERNESS PEOPLE
Cavemen and Forest Folk

If you and I could go back in time fifteen or twenty *Chapter 1* thousand years, we would be in a world very different from the one in which we live today.

Most of the northern half of the earth was covered with glaciers, or great sheets of ice, some of them over four thousand feet high. The northern part of the United States as well as much of Canada was blanketed in ice, while smaller glaciers sat like caps of snow on top of the Rockies, the Alps, and other high mountain ranges. The Ice Age gripped our planet.

Frozen into the glaciers were millions of tons of the earth's supply of water. There is only a certain amount of water on our planet, and since so much of it was packed into the glaciers, the level of the world's lakes, streams, and oceans was much lower than it is today. A wide land bridge rose above the waves in the Bering Strait and tied America and Asia in one great land mass. What is now the English Channel was dry land, joining England to the European mainland.

The people who lived on earth during the Ice Age were hunters, fishermen, and gatherers of berries, roots, and other wild foods. They made their tools of stone, shell, bone, and wood and their clothing of animal skins and the bark of trees. Moving from place to place in search of food, they built no permanent settlements. The world was an unending wilderness as it had been for millions of years.

In spite of the cold, life was good for the hunting people who lived in Europe. No game could live on the ice sheets, but the frozen plains and swamps just south of the glaciers were crowded with vast herds of mammoth, reindeer, giant bison, woolly rhinoceros, and wild horse. These huge beasts were a walk-

During the short summers, hunting people of the Ice Age made their homes under the overhang of great rocks and cliffs. *In this museum model we see a hunting band preparing hides and making tools of stone and of the bones, antlers, and tusks of animals.*

ing supermarket that gave the hunters not only fresh meat but almost everything they needed for living.

The skins and hides provided them with clothing and shelter. The antlers, bones, and tusks supplied weapons, tools, and other hardware. The teeth became necklaces. In a land without wood, the bones made an excellent fuel for fires. Nothing was wasted.

During the long and severe winters the hunters and their families lived in caves, which they decorated with wall paintings of the animals to which they owed their very life. Winter was also a time for

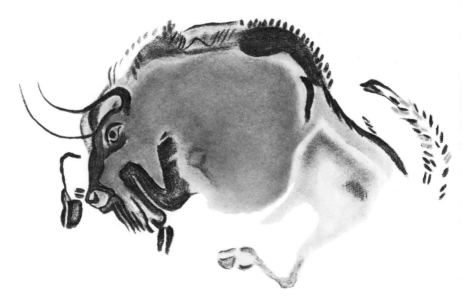

The freezing winters of the Ice Age compelled the hunting people of Europe to live in caves which they decorated with pictures of the great animals that supplied their food, clothing, weapons, and even fuel for their fires. *This giant bison was painted on the walls of the cave at Altamira in Spain about 20,000 years ago.*

making and repairing weapons, preparing furs and skins for clothing, engaging in religious ceremonies, and renewing acquaintances with neighboring bands. But since the animals moved from place to place in search of fresh pasture, the hunters could not settle down permanently.

When summer came and the herds moved on, the hunters had to give up their caves and tag along. How far they traveled and how long they remained in one place depended on the habits of the animals they hunted. They were tied to the herds as closely as wolves that follow the trail of their prey mile after mile and day after day.

To the hunters, however, the wandering life must have seemed a very good one. The climate was cruel and harsh. Yet they had everything they needed: shelter, weapons, warm clothing, and good whole-some food. The game was so plentiful that they had leisure time for dancing, ceremonies, and painting hundreds of pictures on endless cave walls. Why

(left) The wandering of the Ice Age people probably resembled the habits of some present-day Eskimos. As the cold Arctic winter comes on, the Eskimos settle down in tiny villages close to good hunting grounds. When spring arrives the villages are deserted and the Eskimos move along the coast searching for seals and birds. During the summer the bands break up into tiny groups to hunt caribou inland. Then as winter returns, village life begins all over again. *Eskimo men fishing at Polly Bay, Northwest Territory, Canada.*

should they not go on living in this way for thousands of years to come?

But then somewhere between twelve and fourteen thousand years ago the climate of the earth began to grow warmer, and the Ice Age gradually drew to an end. Though the increase in temperature amounted to only a few degrees it was enough to melt the great ice sheets that had kept almost half the earth in cold storage. As the glaciers melted, they released tremendous quantities of water and raised the level of the seas around the world. The land bridge that had joined Asia and America was submerged under the waters of the Bering Strait. England became an island separated from the mainland of Europe by the waters of the English Channel. Oceans, seas, continents, and islands throughout the world began to look the way they do today.

The ending of the Ice Age had a tremendous effect on the life of the cave hunters. The warming of the earth turned the frozen plains and swamps of Europe into forest land and destroyed the low-lying cold weather plants on which the big herd animals had fed. Deprived of their food supply, the mammoth, giant bison, and rhinoceros died out. The reindeer drifted north to the Arctic, where it can still be found today.

Once the Ice Age animals were gone, the hunters had to find other sources of food. Giving up their

Today in far corners of our planet a few primitive people continue to live on wild food just as all mankind did more than ten thousand years ago. *Near Darwin in the Northern Territory of Australia men haul a huge turtle into a dugout canoe.*

caves, some of the hunters wandered to the shore of the sea, where they fished and gathered shellfish and whatever else the tide threw their way. Others, whom we call the forest folk, made their home in the new woodlands of Europe, where they gathered wild plants and chased the deer and boar.

To help them in their hunting, the forest folk invented the bow and arrow, a weapon that was especially useful against the swift-moving creatures of the

Deer Hu
Castellon-S

Though the Ice Age was over, people continued to live as hunt-ers and gatherers relying on what they could kill or pick up in the wilderness. About ten thousand years ago a hunter painted this picture of a deer hunt on a rock wall in Spain. Unlike the Ice Age hunters who used spears and spear throwers, these forest folk hunted with bows and arrows.

wood. They also tamed the wild dog to track down birds and animals hidden in the underbrush. Long before sheep, goats, or cows were domesticated, the dog had become man's hunting companion and pet.

In addition to the bow and arrow the forest folk made a number of other clever inventions, including skis, sleds, boats, paddles, harpoons, and fishing hooks. Yet we cannot say that their way of life was an improvement over that of the Ice Age hunters. The great ice sheets had vanished, the climate was very pleasant, and green forests covered the land. Still the forest folk lived a difficult kind of life searching for small game and gathering berries, seeds, roots, snails, and insects to satisfy their hunger. The great steak barbecues of the cavemen were long forgotten.

The Ice Age had come and gone, and man remained what his ancestors had been for hundreds of thousands of years: a wanderer without a fixed home, relying on what he chanced to kill or pick up in the wilderness. Like those who had lived before him, he continued to make his rude tools of stone, bone, wood, and shell and his clothing of animal skins and bark. In many ways he lived no better than the animals on which he preyed.

A hunter and gatherer of wild food, he built no cities, towns, or villages. Neither did he clear the land for planting or dig beneath the surface for metals. Wandering through the wilderness, he disturbed the face of nature no more than if a pack of animals had passed through. His mark on the earth was slight.

Our powerful modern machines can tear down great forests, level hillsides, or change the course of rivers. The tools of early man, however, were powered only by human strength and could make little change in the environment. *This tribesman of western Australia whose life is like that of an ancient hunter is cutting a tree with a crude tool made of wood and stone.*

Although it first appeared in the Middle East, farming was also discovered by the Indians of America. The early farmers of Central and South America probably lived in villages similar to this settlement of Yagua Indians in Colombia, South America, today.

THE DISCOVERY OF FARMING
Sickles, Pets, and Wild Cattle

Chapter 2 At the end of the Ice Age hunting people discovered a new way of obtaining their food. Instead of wandering about the wilderness searching for wild plants and animals, they stayed close to home and lived on the crops they grew and the animals they raised. Hunters became farmers.

Farming was first discovered in the Middle East, the region south and east of the Mediterranean Sea that stretched all the way from Egypt to Turkey and Iran. It was, for the most part, a hot dry country with barren mountains and great deserts. In some places, however, there were fertile river valleys, green oases, and lofty hillsides with enough rainfall to attract a wide variety of plants and animals.

The Middle East was also the home of wild cattle, sheep, goats, and pigs, the very animals that could be tamed and domesticated. It was, in addition, the home of wild wheat and barley, two of the most important crops farmers raise today. In the Middle East, nature was ready to provide just the animals and plants man needed to become a farmer and raise his own food.

Among those hunting people who took the first steps toward farming were the Natufians, a group of *About 12,000 Years Ago* small hunting bands that lived in Israel and Lebanon along the eastern shore of the Mediterranean Sea. Though some of the Natufians were cave dwellers, others lived in sturdily built stone houses. Now since it is not likely that people are going to take the trouble to build stone houses unless they intend to spend a good deal of time in them, we have to conclude that the Natufians had given up their wandering life and settled down, at least for a good part of the year. They were still hunters and gatherers, and yet they had a home address.

In addition, we know that these hunters used sickles, or harvesting knives, a sign that they were cutting down some kind of grain, possibly wheat or bar-

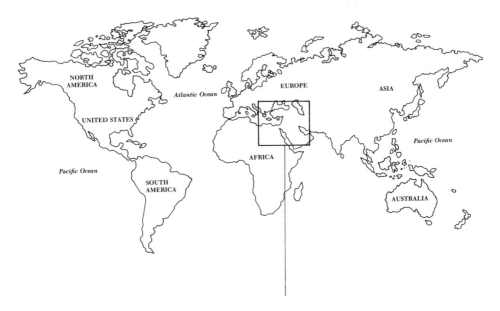

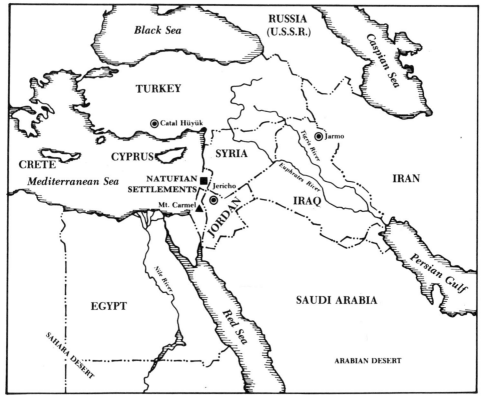

ley. Now if a part of their food supply was grain, we can understand how they were able to settle down. Unlike meat, which spoils quickly, grain could be safely stored away for many months. With good food available at home, the Natufians had less need to wander about than other hunting and gathering people.

You will notice that I have not said that the Natufians were *raising* their own grain. The wheat and barley they cut down with their sickles were wild varieties that they came upon in the wilderness, just as they found roots, berries, and nuts. They were still hunters and gatherers of wild food—not farmers. On the other hand we can't be sure that they were not planting a few of the seeds they brought home or even taming a wild goat or two.

These little hunting bands apparently were on the verge of farming. Halfway people, they lived by hunting and gathering very much as their ancestors

THE BEGINNING OF FARMING (left)

Hunting and gathering bands turned to farming about ten thousand years ago in the Middle East. As it happened, this region was the home of wild plants and animals that could be domesticated by man such as wheat and barley, and cattle, sheep, and goats. Among the very first farming communities were Jericho, Jarmo, and Catal Hüyük. From the Middle East, farming spread to many parts of the Old World.

In America, however, the Indians discovered farming by themselves without any help from the settlers of Asia, Africa, or Europe.

If all men had continued to live as hunters and gatherers, there would be no cities today, no books or scientific advances. Until they could discover another way of getting their food, people were doomed to be what their ancestors had been for a million years—wanderers whose existence depended on finding wild animals and plants. About the time the Ice Age came to an end, however, hunters and gatherers in Southwest Asia discovered that they could raise their own crops and domesticate animals. *A group of women cultivating rice in India today.*

had for many thousands of years. But at the same time they built sturdy homes for themselves, stored food from season to season, and, quite possibly, experimented with raising a few plants and animals. They seem to have been building a bridge between the settled life of the farmer and the wandering life of the hunter and gatherer.

Unfortunately, we know little about the actual steps that led ancient people from hunting and gathering to growing their own crops and raising their own animals. You will remember that we are looking back to a time long before men learned to write and record their history. We may carefully explore the ruins of a tiny settlement with its bits of stone sickles and refuse of charred seeds and animal bones. Yet we often don't know whether we are looking at a camp of hunters or a village of farmers.

Were the sickles used to cut down wild or domesticated wheat? Were the bones those of wild sheep that hunters had killed, or were the bones those of domestic sheep that farmers had raised? Often it is impossible to tell. Though we use all the help we can get from the archaeologists who have dug into the ancient settlements, we still have a lot of guessing to do.

We may imagine a band of Middle Eastern hunters coming upon a patch of wild wheat in the wilderness. Instead of just walking by as they had formerly done, they decided to take care of it. To help the young green plants along, they pulled up the weeds. They chased deer or other grazing animals away and put up a scarecrow to frighten off the birds.

We see these hunting people relating to nature in a new way. They were no longer merely gathering wild plants as their ancestors had done. They were now protecting them and encouraging their growth. They were behaving toward these wild plants as a farmer does toward his own domesticated plants.

We believe that it was the women in ancient hunting bands and not the men who discovered how to raise plants. In this picture, a woman in western Australia is grinding seeds gathered in the wilderness into flour. Even if the men should come home from the hunt with no game at all, no one in the band will go hungry.

At harvest time we imagine the hunters proudly carrying home more grain than they had ever collected before. A few of the kernels falling on the garbage heap of the settlement soon took root and sprouted. The thought then came to some in the band that they could help nature along by scattering seeds themselves. Instead of poking about in the wild looking for grain, they could produce a whole field of grain right outside their door.

The next step was the deliberate planting of seeds. It was one of the greatest experiments of all time, for it led mankind out of the wilderness into village life and finally to civilization.

The women in the band and not the men were probably the first farmers. Because they were in charge of gathering seeds, berries, roots, and wild fruits, they knew far more about plants than did the men. While the men were away hunting, fishing, or just loafing, the women were conducting the great experiments that opened the way to farming.

We can only imagine how hunting people learned to domesticate farm animals. Making pets of wild animals must have been one of the ways. We can picture a hunter coming home with a wild lamb he caught nibbling away at the family wheat patch. Since he already had a supply of grain on hand, he did not have to slaughter the young animal for food. Instead, he turned it over to his children for feeding and training. The young animal grew up as a household pet, and later became the first member of a domesticated flock of sheep.

We cannot, however, imagine wild cattle, which are among the strongest and most dangerous of beasts, becoming household pets. They were probably captured by being driven into a corral, where the larger and fiercer animals were killed at once. The smaller and gentler animals were saved and raised in a fenced-in pasture. In this way over a long period of time, tame varieties of cattle were bred which could be milked and used to carry packs and pull carts.

The earliest farming experimenters did not know what you and I know today: that only *certain* wild animals could be domesticated. They therefore tried to raise all sorts of odd creatures. Thousands of years after the first animals were domesticated farmers were still trying to tame the untamable. A picture found on the walls of an Egyptian tomb shows farmers feeding hyenas in a barn just as though they were cattle. It was a good try but it must have failed for we don't know of any farmers who are raising hyenas today.

The experiments with cattle, sheep, pigs, and goats, however, succeeded so well that these species have become the principal domesticated animals of the Western world. Today we continue to raise the same species of animals that Middle Eastern hunters tamed over ten thousand years ago.

At the end of the Ice Age, hunters and gatherers in the Middle East were beginning to change the environment in which they lived. They took wild plants and animals out of the wilderness and moved them into the safety of their settlements, where they tamed and domesticated them. For the first time in history men were relocating the natural resources of the earth.

About 10,000 Years Ago The change from hunting and gathering wild food to farming has been called the Agricultural Revolution. But we should not think of it as a sudden change in the life of man. A hunter did not wake one morning, break his bow and arrows over his knee, and begin to scatter seeds over his fields. The change was gradual and extended over many lifetimes. It was the result not of one grand discovery but of a long series of modest little happenings, such as scattering seed over the garbage heap outside the door or letting the children make a pet of a frightened wild lamb instead of carving it up for supper.

And once people became farmers they did not give up hunting and gathering. For many hundreds of years the yield from their little fields of grain and

When ancient farmers began to raise plants and animals they did not give up wild food. While the women did the farm work, the men continued to hunt and fish. Today millions of people all over the world, including ourselves, still get a good portion of their food from the seas and inland waterways. *A fisherman in Dahomey, Africa, casts his net upon the waters of Lake Ahemé.*

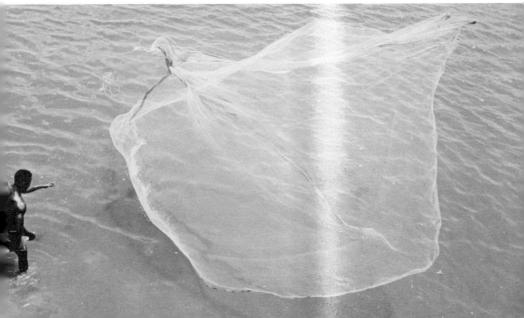

their half-starved, half-wild animals was too skimpy to provide for their growing families. While their wives took care of the farm work the men continued to go off into the wild to hunt, fish, and gather wild food. Even today in a world of supermarkets, deep freezers, and packaged foods, we sometimes go off into the country to fish and collect mushrooms, birds' eggs, nuts, berries, and whatever else wild nature throws our way. A little of the hunter and gatherer lingers in all of us.

Only after they had settled down to village life did men build sturdy year-round houses. Making far greater use of the environment than did their hunting ancestors, they took the soft clay of the river shore and transformed it into pottery, tools, and building material. *In Chad, Africa, farmers build a new family house with clay.*

THREE EARLY VILLAGES
Pots, Skulls, and Vultures

A thousand years or so after hunters and gatherers began their experiments with plants and animals, the first farming villages of mankind arose in the Middle East. *Chapter 3*

One of the oldest of these villages was Jarmo in the hill country of northern Iraq, a pleasant land of temperate climate and rainfall. In their little fields the farmers of Jarmo grew wheat, barley, lentils, beans, and peas: everything you'd want for a good thick vegetable soup. They harvested their grain with *About 9,000 Years Ago* stone-toothed sickles and ground it into flour in stone mortars. To add variety to their meals they gathered acorns and pistachio nuts in the woods and hunted wild pig, sheep, and cattle.

Like their hunting ancestors the farmers of Jarmo were Stone Age people who made their tools and weapons of stone. But unlike their ancestors they were also making use of clay. They used clay to make images of their gods, toys for their children, and a full line of kitchenware, including pots, pans, ladles, bowls, and cups.

The increasing use of clay by the early farmer tells us that people were taking greater advantage of the

Because they wandered from place to place in search of wild food, early hunters had no need of permanent dwellings. They often made temporary shelters of hides, leaves, and twigs. *A temporary hut set up by Bushmen of South Africa, among the few people left on earth who have no fixed home.*

resources of the environment. To the hunter clay was only a soft formless ooze on the edge of the river. In the hands of the farmer it became a hard, water-proof, and often beautiful container, statue, or vase. The farmer found treasures in the earth of which the hunter had never dreamed.

Farmers prospered in the temperate hill country around Jarmo. Yet they could do equally well in surroundings that were quite different. Five hundred miles to the southwest of Jarmo is the Dead Sea Valley of Palestine. Nine hundred feet below sea level, it is one of the hottest and dreariest places on earth. In the heart of the valley, however, there is a fertile oasis called Jericho, which is fed by an underground spring that has been flowing since the end of the Ice Age.

About eleven thousand years ago a band of Natufian hunters stumbled upon the oasis. They built a few crude huts and settled down to living very much like their cousins on the Mediterranean coast. When in the course of time their huts collapsed they built new ones right over the ruins so that they could remain close to the spring. As the years went by and as each generation kept building over older shelters, an artificial hill arose that soared above the oasis. Such man-made mounds, which are found all over the Middle East, are called *tells*.

The tell at Jericho is now over seventy feet high, and when you see it for the first time, covered with weeds and bushes, you'll probably mistake it for a natural hill. But dig into it and you will strike crumbling walls, fragments of tools and weapons, bits of pottery, and other refuse, all left by the people who lived here for thousands of years. It is man's first giant junk pile.

The Natufian hunters lived at Jericho for one thousand years, and then a huge farming community took their place on the tell. The inhabitants lived in comfortable, well-designed houses with good-sized storage closets and spacious rooms that opened on a central courtyard. They must have taken a great deal of pride in their homes, for the floors were covered with a hard highly polished surface.

These tidy householders had a curious burial custom. They plastered human features on the skulls of their dead and replaced the eyes with seashells. They then buried the skulls under the floor of their homes, probably as a safeguard against misfortune. If that is the case, the skulls did a good job, for the villagers prospered and lived at peace for many years.

Because the original oasis was far too small to provide the food needed by a large community, the villagers must have made use of irrigation just as the people who live in Jericho do today. By digging ditches and channels they allowed the water of the

In ancient Jericho in the Middle East nine thousand years ago, the early farmers learned to turn the barren desert into fertile fields. Today irrigation is employed all over the world. *On this Mexican farm, water is brought to the fields by a ditch and siphoned between the rows of crops.*

In the far western United States, vast sections of the desert have been transformed into farmlands by means of irrigation. *This aerial view of the Coachella Valley in California shows how the desert was changed after irrigation with water from the Colorado River.*

spring to flow into the surrounding desert. In this way they turned the barren sands into fertile soil for their crops.

The farmer changed wild plants into cultivated grains, savage beasts into gentle farmyard animals, and river mud into pottery. Now we see him changing the landscape, transforming sandy wastes into green and luxuriant gardens. The first architect of the outdoors, he rearranged and reshaped the environment to his own design.

The early farmers of Jericho made their tools and weapons of stone, which could be picked up in the neighborhood of their village. But they were also, like farmers elsewhere, beginning to use obsidian, a tough jet-black natural glass that came from the volcanic mountains of central Turkey.

Eighty-five hundred years ago there was a farming settlement in central Turkey called Catal Hüyük. Today all that you can see of Catal is a tremendous mound of ruins. But at the beginning of the Agricultural Revolution it was the largest and richest community in the world, owing its wealth to the obsidian it exported to all parts of the Middle East.

Catal Hüyük was an almost solid mass of attached one-story houses that looked somewhat like the pueblos of the American Indians of our Southwest. There were no streets, and all moving about, therefore, took place over the housetops. A householder en-

The settlement of Catal Hüyük in Turkey eighty-five hundred years ago probably resembled the pueblos of the American Indians of the Southwest. Like the ancient inhabitants of Catal a Pueblo Indian enters his home by climbing down a ladder which extends from an opening in the roof. *The present-day pueblo of San Juan, New Mexico.*

tered his home not through a door but by climbing down a ladder from an opening in the roof.

Like the people of Jericho, the Catalians buried their dead within their houses. The bodies of the dead were first exposed in the open air, where the flesh was probably devoured by vultures. Several magnificent paintings that have been found in the ruins of Catal show these birds pecking away at corpses. Once the bodies had been stripped of all flesh, the skeletons were laid to rest in the houses under platforms on which the members of the family slept. No one seems to have worried about ghosts.

The people of Catal must have believed in a life

after death, for they buried the dead with a large variety of funeral gifts to keep them busy and well fed in the other world. These gifts ranged all the way from cosmetics, mirrors, jewelry, belts, daggers, and arrowheads to eggs, fruits, and beef roasts. Long before the birth of our modern religions, mankind believed that the dead would live again.

Catal Hüyük as well as Jarmo and Jericho speak to us across the centuries. They show us how quickly people could develop a new and better way of living once they learned to grow their own food. Within two thousand years after hunters had succeeded in coaxing a few miserable patches of grain out of the ground and milking a few scrawny goats, their crude camps were replaced by permanent villages where people lived in comfortable homes, developed art and religion, and traded with distant places. People whose forefathers had ranged through the wilderness in tiny bands now lived close to their neighbors in a year-round community that held thousands of inhabitants.

You and I are so used to obtaining our food from domesticated plants and animals that we take farming for granted. But to a hunter who wandered into an early farming village in the Middle East, farming must have been as miraculous as the first voyage into space was for us.

The villagers seemed able to feed themselves without stirring far from their front door. While the hunter and his band scurried about in the wilderness poking under the bark of trees for larvae and grubs or chasing after game, these farmers were harvesting grain in a nearby field. Though the hunter was a skillful and tireless woodsman, there were times when the fish did not bite, his trap did not spring, and his arrow missed its mark. Whether he and his family ate or not depended not so much on his hard work as on luck or accident.

Farmers, on the other hand, having planted a crop, usually reaped a harvest. And even when a crop failed they could fall back on the grain they had stored away. They had more food than the hunter had, and they could rely on its being there when it was needed.

When the hunter and his band remained in one neighborhood for a time they exhausted all the wild plant and animal food in the vicinity. That was one reason they had to keep moving from place to place. But when the farmer settled down in one place he did not use up his food supply. Instead of disappearing, his flocks and herds grew larger. He knew how to eat his cake and have it too.

The hunter gazed in wonder as the farmer's wife turned the muddy clay of the river into glistening pottery or spun cloth out of flax or cotton. What must have astonished him most of all was his first sight of sheep with coats of wool. The wild sheep he hunted had hairy coats like deer. He did not know that the farmers had been able to breed a wool-bearing variety from wild sheep.

Both the Middle Eastern hunter and the farmer inhabited the same environment. Yet the farmer, because of his discoveries, inventions, and tools, was able to take far greater advantage of the environment than did the hunter. The farmer was the magician of the environment who could take the raw materials of nature and turn them into useful treasures.

Today, in the very same land where the Indians once hunted and raised crops in wilderness clearings, we build great cities and towns. The physical surroundings of people influence their way of living. Yet people can relate to their surroundings in very different ways.

We may not know what went on in the minds of the hunters who came into contact with the early farmers. But we do know that wherever farmers went they converted hunting bands to their way of life. Within a few thousand years of the first Natufian experiments, farming had reached the far corners of the Middle East and was ready to spread out in triumph into other parts of the world.

Wherever they wandered the pioneering farmers of the Middle East took their domesticated plants and animals along with them. In this way wheat, barley, cattle, sheep, and goats reached the continent of Europe. Thousands of years later when the European colonists came to America they brought their plants and animals. Man takes a part of his environment with him wherever he goes. *The ancestors of this American dairy herd originally came from the Middle East.*

THE EUROPEAN PIONEERS

A Few Seeds and a Farm Animal or Two

Once the farming way of life had taken hold in the **Chapter 4** Middle East, it continued to travel until it covered almost all of the Old World from North Africa in the West to China in the Far East.

About seven thousand years ago farming colonists spilled out of the Middle East and set up their villages in the great trackless forests of Europe. They made clearings in the woods and planted their grain among the tree stumps. After a few years, however, they discovered that their crops were failing. Forest soil contains little nourishment for hungry plants such as wheat and barley and quickly loses its fertility. All the colonists could do was to give up their fields and villages and go off in search of fresh soil.

Some of the colonists tried to enrich the soil by means of "slash and burn." They killed the trees by slashing a ring around the bark. Then after the trees dried, they burned them down and planted seeds in the ashes, which were rich in the minerals needed by plants.

"Slash and burn" seemed to work for the first crop was successful, and the second was almost as good. But the time soon came when the soil again lost its fertility. The farmers were forced to move on, bag and baggage, to another part of the forest where they started slashing and burning all over again. I think you can see what happened. Leaving a trail of deserted villages behind them, the farmers kept wandering through the wilderness until they reached the northern regions of the continent.

I do not have to tell you that no one farming band ever made the complete two thousand mile journey from the Middle East to, let us say, Norway or Sweden. During his lifetime a farmer probably moved no more than one or two hundred miles from the village in which he was born. As long as fertile soil was avail-

Humans lived on the planet for hundreds of thousands of years before they discovered how to raise plants and domesticate animals. Up to the time man became a farmer, he had only been a part of the landscape. Now he began to change the environment, turning the wilderness into gardens, pasture, irrigated fields, and villages.

We call the period before farming the Old Stone Age, and the period just after, the New Stone Age. The chart shows the approximate time farming started in different parts of the world.

THE OLD STONE AGE

A Million Years of Hunting and Gathering

THE BEGINNING OF FARMING
AND THE NEW STONE AGE

Thousands of Years Ago	Southwest Asia	Egypt	China	Europe	Indonesia	The Americas
10,000						
9,000						
8,000						
7,000						
6,000						
5,000						
4,000						
3,000						
2,000						
1,000						

able around his settlement he tended his crops and stayed on. When good soil became scarce he and his fellow villagers pulled up stakes and pushed deeper into the wilderness.

In those far-off days before the beginning of civilization, people had plenty of elbow room in which to move around. Land was free for the taking, and there were no fences, "keep off" signs, or border police. The entire continent was open to exploration and settlement.

The native forest folk, who had been living in Europe since the end of the Ice Age, seemed to offer little resistance. We think that they remained on friendly terms with the strangers from the south. Instead of fighting, the forest folk probably traded with the colonists, exchanging game for farm products. Some, seeing the advantages of raising plants and animals, became farmers themselves.

The forest folk may have felt toward the wandering farmers as the Indians felt toward the white explorers of America five thousand years later. Lewis and Clark, the explorers of the Far West, were able to travel through Indian territory all the way from the Mississippi to the Pacific Ocean without interference. They were welcomed by the Indians almost everywhere they went and helped on their way with guides and supplies. Today the path Lewis and Clark followed in 1806 is barred by thousands of gates, walls, and "no trespassing" notices.

The time came when the wandering farmers did settle down permanently. The fortunate discovery of a complete ancient village at Köln Lindenthal near the city of Cologne in Germany gives us a picture of how some of the colonists ended their wandering life.

Originally a band of "slash and burn" farmers built a sturdy village at Köln Lindenthal, consisting of twenty-one long wooden houses arranged in rows and surrounded by a low fence. The village resembled the settlements of the Iroquois Indians in America before 1776. Like the Europeans, the Iroquois also were "slash and burn" farmers.

About ten years after building the village, the farmers of Köln Lindenthal packed up and moved away. Sometime later, however, unlike other wandering farmers, they returned. Several years went by, and once again they deserted the village and once again returned. Each time they returned, they rebuilt the village making slight changes in the arrangement of the houses. Only after they had gone away and come back several more times did they at last settle down for good.

What led them to end their wandering days?

The Köln Lindenthalers had abandoned their village when their crops failed. They returned, however, when they found out that the forest had regrown over their deserted fields. They then burned down the new growth and planted their crops in the soil enriched by the ashes.

The farmers had discovered that they could use the same land over and over again if they only gave the forest time enough to regrow. Whey then should they abandon their village? Instead of wandering about in search of new soil they could stay at home and shift or rotate their crops from field to field every few years.

There was still another way to keep the soil fertile.

The early hunter left the natural landscape very much as he found it. The farmer reshaped and rearranged it to suit his needs. Farms took the place of wild forest, the course of rivers was changed, swamplands were drained, and land was reclaimed from the sea. By remodeling the surface of the earth, farmers have virtually created works of art. *In Clayton County, Iowa, the surface of the earth has been reshaped in vast swirls or contours which help to preserve the soil and water on sloping ground.*

The European farmers slowly became aware that the fields on which their cattle, sheep, and goats had grazed continued to yield large harvests even after many plantings. The manure of farm animals proved to be an excellent fertilizer. It put back into the soil essential minerals that growing crops took from it.

People who settle down get to know their environment far better than those who just wander around. It was not long before some of the farmers discovered that there were valuable resources not only on the surface of the earth but deep within the earth. Throughout Europe farmers became miners.

At Windmill Hill in southern England, for example, farmers sank a deep shaft into the earth to obtain flint, the sturdy stone they used for tools and weapons. From the bottom of the shaft, forty feet below the surface of the earth, they gouged out long horizontal tunnels, leaving limestone pillars to support the overwhelming weight of the earth above. It is startling to learn that they had only the crudest kind of equipment for their work: shovels made of pig and ox shoulder bones and picks made of deer antler. For Stone Age people, whose grandparents had wandered across the face of Europe from one temporary settlement to another, the mine at Windmill Hill was a remarkable engineering achievement.

Up to this time in his history man, whether hunter or farmer, had only skimmed the surface of the earth.

Now he was beginning to explore the environment underground. Someday the descendants of those who tunneled beneath the surface of the earth at Windmill Hill would dive to the bottom of the sea and climb the reaches of the upper air.

The spread of farming throughout Europe is one of the great success stories of mankind. The Middle Eastern pioneers who boldly plunged into the uncharted wilderness with only a pouch of seeds and a farm animal or two seemed to have all the odds against them at first. They never knew when they might be surprised and killed by the mysterious forest folk through whose lands they passed.

Nor did they know whether the plants and animals they brought with them from the sun-drenched hills and river valleys of the Middle East would survive in a cool northern climate. Wheat and barley as well as cattle, sheep, and goats were unknown in Europe until the farmers arrived.

The pioneers were fortunate. The forest folk they encountered were peaceful, and the crops and animals they brought with them thrived in the new environment. Even their wandering way of life turned out to be an advantage. By moving on every few years they gave the land a chance to grow back into forest and regain its fertility. When they finally did settle down they kept the soil from becoming exhausted by using animal manure and shifting their crops from field to field. Today after seven thousand years of farming, Europe still has some of the richest farming land on earth.

The Middle Eastern farmers who paddled across the Mediterranean tamed the wilderness without destroying the land. Far from their birthplace in the sun-drenched oases and river valleys of Southwest Asia and Northern Africa, they raised the plants and animals they had brought with them. Moving slowly through the trackless forests in small bands, they gradually transformed the European continent into a land of park-like woods, broad meadows, gardens, and farms.

People can be good to the environment.

The farmer-colonists of the Middle East gradually transformed the European wilderness. Today it still has some of the most fertile farmland on earth. *The rich fields of Herefordshire in England.*

Beginning about seven thousand years ago small bands of wandering farmers from southwestern Asia and northern Africa boldly made their way into the mysterious European wilderness. Avoiding serious fighting with the native forest folk they enjoyed longer periods of peace than civilized man has known since. *Model of a village founded by Stone Age farmers in Denmark about five thousand years ago. You will notice that there are no walls or fortifications around the settlement.*

WHEN ALL MEN AND WOMEN WERE EQUAL
Cousins, Sharers, and Spirits

Chapter 5 If you could travel back six thousand years in time and visit an early farming village, the first thing you would probably notice would be the small size of the community. Today we cluster together in gigantic cities teeming with millions of people. But in the days before civilization, people lived in settlements so small that everyone knew everyone else. A typical village held no more than two hundred people.

A village was a band of relatives. A man lived in the

company of parents, brothers and sisters, uncles and aunts, and a multitude of cousins near and distant. In the course of his entire lifetime he probably never came upon anyone to whom he was not related in some way.

Everything in his village was more important to him, and better known, than any person or thing in the outside world. Once beyond the village gate, there was no one he could rely on, no one he could turn to. Only in his village did he feel safe and happy. His village was his world.

Although an early village was a very small place, it could get along without any help from the outside. Everything a villager needed was within walking distance. His grain grew in a little plot outside his door, and his cattle grazed in a nearby pasture. He fished and hunted in the neighboring forest and picked up clay and stone on the bank of a nearby stream. If all trade with the outside world were cut off, he might grumble about the loss of obsidian for his tools, but he and his fellow villagers would survive.

Today we could not get along without the services of all sorts of special workers, including the postman, the corner butcher, the doctor, and the TV repairman. The early farmer, however, managed all the tasks of living by himself. He was a jack-of-all-trades as skillful in building a canoe or slaughtering a goat as in making his clothing or polishing a flint axe.

The archaeologists who have dug into the ruins of the ancient villages tell us that the houses were generally of the same size and furnished in the same way. Where were the homes of the wealthy or the powerful? Evidently such people did not exist in the early villages. There were no rich or poor, masters or slaves, nobles or commoners. Economically each man was the equal of his neighbor, doing the same kind of work and owning about the same amount of property. The chief himself was no wealthier than the rest of his people and hunted and fished and took care of his farm just as everyone else did.

We may think of a Stone Age chieftain as a terrifying figure with the power of life and death over his people. Still, if he was anything like the headman among many primitive people living today he actually had very little authority. Important decisions were probably made not by the chief but by a council of elders or an assembly of all the men and women in the community.

In a primitive village today a headman is expected to be a sort of kindly grandfather who gives presents to his people and hands out good advice and guidance. If he is smart he will give orders only to the children because he knows that the adults will pay no attention. Among some South American Indians in the Amazon, it is said that when the chief commands it is the signal for everyone to do as he pleases.

In the early villages women held a great deal of power and influence because the welfare of the community depended on their farming skills. During the Ice Age they had occupied an inferior position in society since they did not have the muscular strength to kill big game. When farming began, however, they became the breadwinners and the equals of the men.

We do not know if woman's important position in the early villages helped to prevent war but there is remarkably little evidence of large-scale fighting during the New Stone Age. The huge settlement of Catal Hüyük lived at peace for over eight hundred years. At Köln Lindenthal the original colonists felt so safe from attack that they built no stockades or fortifications around their forest village. One reason that peace prevailed in the early villages may be that women helped make the decisions.

Not only was there peace between villages. There was little conflict within villages. And with free land available elsewhere, those who did not get along with their neighbors could always go off and begin their own communities rather than quarrel at home. To judge by life in primitive farming communities in our own time, people led very orderly lives although there were no police, judges, or prisons. An early village must have been a far safer place than many of our modern cities.

Although people lived by rules quite different

from ours, they had as strong a sense of right and wrong as we have. One of their most important obligations was generosity toward neighbors. When there were bad times everyone was expected to help out. When there were good times everyone shared. A man could not sit down to a feast knowing that a neighbor was hungry. In many villages there was a public granary or storehouse in which all the families kept their grain and from which any family could draw anytime they were in need of food.

Hospitality is a strong custom among many primitive people. When Columbus landed in America he was so amazed by the kindness and generosity of the Indians that he imagined that he had discovered the Garden of Eden.

A villager owned his personal possessions such as weapons, clothing, and household goods. He did not own the land on which he farmed. The land was usually the property of the entire community or of a group of families which lent it to the farmer. If a farmer stopped working his farm he had to return it to the community. It was therefore impossible for any individual to become rich by keeping a lot of land for himself.

Today a fisherman may go to jail for fishing in a stream belonging to someone else. But during the days of the early villages all were free to make use of the resources of nature. Everyone could go into the

Our ancient hunting and farming ancestors lived in a deep silence broken only by such natural sounds as the cry of wild animals and birds or the rushing of a waterfall. But we who live in the modern cities are constantly exposed to the whine of machinery, the whirr and screech of traffic, and the roar of airplanes overhead. Modern man is the noisiest creature that has ever lived. *A waterfall in Glacier National Park, Montana.*

woodlands and hunt, fish, and pick up timber, stone, clay, and whatever else he needed. All men were equal because all had an equal opportunity to make use of the treasures of the environment.

The early farmers thought of nature as they thought of their fellow human beings. Rivers, trees, and mountains were not things as they are to us but living spirits under the protection of their gods.

The Mayan Indians of Central America, who were also Stone Age farmers, could not clear the forests in order to plant their corn until they had addressed the gods in this way:

> Oh God, My Father, My Mother,
> Lord of the Hills,
> Spirit of the Forest.
> Be patient with me.
> Be understanding.
> If I cut down the trees,
> It is only that I may live.

Today we could not possibly imagine a lumber company begging the permission of the gods to cut down thousands of acres of woodland with its powerful machines. But in the days of the ancient farmers the environment was sacred.

The gods gave people permission to make use of the soil, the water, the air, the plants, and the animals. But people, on the other hand, were never to abuse the resources of nature. In those far-off days the water was fit to drink and the air was fit to breathe. The constellations blazed in the clear night sky and the land was unspoiled.

Man's mark on the earth was gentle.

The early farmers could rely only on their own muscles and hand tools. They probably had the same kind of simple equipment as these workmen in Java, Indonesia, who are carrying loads of earth and clay to build an irrigation canal.

THE COMING OF THE CITY

Waterworks, Plows, and Warriors

Six thousand years ago the farming way of life had **Chapter 6** triumphed over the way of the hunter and gatherer.

All over the Old World, from North Africa in the West to China in the Far East, prosperous farmers were raising crops and domesticated animals. Hunting people were abandoning their age-old pursuit of wild food and settling down to village life. Only in the frozen North and in remote jungles, deserts, and mountain fastnesses did wandering bands hold to

47

their ancient ways, as some of them do to this day.

Tough and independent, the hard-working farmers found almost everything they needed for the good life just outside their door. Surrounded by their kinsmen, they dwelled in small democratic communities without rich or poor, nobles or commoners, slaves or masters. Avoiding serious conflict, they lived in harmony with nature as they did with their fellow villagers.

Yet these little self-reliant societies lasted only a short time, and they quickly crumbled away when the first cities of mankind arose a little more than five thousand years ago.

The first cities were built in Mesopotamia, "The Land Between the Rivers," in the heart of the Middle East. At first sight Mesopotamia seemed an unlikely place for any kind of settlement. Most of it was a barren desert as flat as a baseball field. Two great rivers, however, the Tigris and Euphrates, flowed through the land, leaving tracts of fertile soil along the shorelines and along the swamp region that jutted out into the Persian Gulf.

The first settlers who came from the hill country near Jarmo in northern Iraq built their villages on the edge of the rivers, where nature provided them with almost all the necessities of life. Fish were plentiful. Clay scooped up from the shore made excellent pottery, fishhooks, axe heads, and sickles. The reeds that grew abundantly in the swamps were bundled together for the construction of houses and boats. You might think twice about trusting yourself to a reed boat; yet you will recall that a few years ago Thor Heyerdahl, the Norwegian anthropologist, safely navigated a boat made of reeds all the way across the Atlantic.

The settlers took full advantage of the rich river environment. In their little garden plots along the shore they grew wheat, barley, and dates and raised cattle, sheep, goats, and pigs. The soil was so rich that they often harvested as many as three crops a year. With plenty of food available the farmers had large families, and the population rapidly increased. It wasn't long before the villages became overcrowded, and all the good farming land on the banks of the rivers was taken.

Elsewhere when land became scarce, some of the inhabitants left home and went off to establish new settlements, one village giving birth to another. The farmers who lived along the Tigris and Euphrates, however, found another solution: they cut irrigation ditches from the rivers into the surrounding desert and created new farmland on the edge of their settlements. Instead of going off and establishing new villages they enlarged their old villages.

As the population of Mesopotamia continued to grow, irrigation canals were pushed further and further into the desert until they intermingled in a complex network of waterways that penetrated every corner of the land. The farmers of Jericho had enlarged an oasis, but the villagers of Mesopotamia transformed a barren desert country into one of the most fertile regions on earth. It was man's most remarkable remodeling of the landscape since the day he became a farmer.

You can guess what was going to happen in the little villages in "The Land Between the Rivers." With so much good farmland close to home, no one was going to leave home, and the villages would continue to grow larger and larger. People were going to live together not in tiny bands or small villages but in vast settlements holding thousands and tens of thousands of inhabitants. The first cities of mankind were about to be born.

About the time that the Mesopotamians began to push their irrigation canals into the desert, they discovered the need for strong leadership. In the early villages people got along quite well without powerful rulers. Villagers who went off by themselves or in small groups to hunt or tend their gardens did not need anyone to tell them what to do or when to do it. A man fishing by himself required no boss.

Irrigation, however, was no one-man or small-group activity. It was a large-scale public works proj-

The early farmers were architects of the outdoors. In Mesopotamia they turned the desert into fertile fields. Elsewhere they remodeled the face of mountains by means of terracing. After the Inca Indians of Peru were defeated by the Spanish conquerors four hundred years ago, some of them fled to the top of a high peak in the Andes called Machu Picchu. Here they built a secret city and planted their crops on terraces that they cut into the side of the mountain in order to save soil and water. You can get some idea of the difficulty of building these terraces from the steepness of the mountain you see in the background of this picture of Machu Picchu.

ect demanding the cooperative efforts of hundreds of trained laborers. When the call came to repair a leak in a dike wall or remove the mud from an irrigation channel, a farmer could not do as he pleased. If he and his neighbors were to survive he had to give instant and unquestioning obedience to a strong leader.

Today we can build a dam with few workers because we have powerful earth-moving machines. The Stone Age farmers had only the simplest kind of tools which were powered by their own muscles. Building a dam, therefore, required the services of armies of laborers. Men were used like beasts of burden.

In the irrigation societies of Mesopotamia the weak rule of the village headmen and elders gave way to the commands of chieftains who gradually gained more and more authority. Some of them acted not only as superintendents of waterworks but also as priests of the gods. In time of war they led the soldiers into battle. Finally when the first cities arose they became the kings and high priests with the power of life and death over their people.

If rivers could be controlled and made to work for men, so could animals. For hundreds of thousands of years men had been forced to carry their burdens on their back. Now they hit on the idea of piling whatever they had to carry on oxen or hitching oxen to a cart. The idea was simple but the consequences were enormous. People could now travel further and trade far more than they had ever done before. The solitary peddler, bent almost double by the pack on his back, was transformed into the proud driver of a caravan transporting huge cargoes of merchandise across the desert or over distant mountains.

Man had always used animals for food. Now he began to use them for power. No longer a beast of burden, he was started on the road that led to wind and water power and finally, in our time, to the power derived from coal, oil, and the atom. The farmer who first hitched an ox to a cart was the forefather of the locomotive engineer, the jet pilot, and the astronaut.

An ox that pulled a cart could just as well drag a plow over a field. In the early villages farmers had turned over the soil with a hand hoe or a primitive digging stick. Now they discovered that by hitching oxen to a plow they could farm more land and grow more food than they had ever managed in the past.

But while women could easily handle a hoe or digging stick, they could not manage a heavy plow and a team of oxen. They retired to their household duties and kitchen gardens and allowed their husbands to take their place in the fields. But once they were no longer the principal breadwinners of the family, they lost the position of equality they formerly held with men. Today in the Women's Liberation movement, women are struggling to recover the rights and privileges they enjoyed in ancient times.

The plow brought other changes to the early farm-

A plow prepares the soil for planting and sowing by cutting furrows into it and turning it over. Formerly farmers had turned over the soil with a digging stick or a hand hoe. By using cattle or donkeys with a plow they were able to cultivate far more land and raise far larger crops than they ever had in the past. Agriculture, which is the cultivation of broad fields rather than small garden patches, began when man hitched an animal to a plow. *With his two tired donkeys this farmer in Iran is tilling the soil the way his Middle Eastern ancestors did five thousand years ago.*

ing communities. Formerly the farmer had been able to raise only enough food to take care of himself and his family. Now by hitching an animal to a plow, he could raise more food than he needed for himself. He could then use this additional food to pay for the services of special workers such as tool makers, potters, carpenters, and boat builders. It was no longer necessary that every person be a producer of food. Many of the trades, professions, and businesses that we find in the classified pages of our telephone direc-

tory today made their first appearance more than six
thousand years ago in the villages of Mesopotamia.

The farmer could also use his extra food to trade *About 5,500*
for materials and goods he did not produce in his own *Years Ago*
village. Of all the materials imported from the outside world the most prized was copper, the first
metal used by man to make tools and weapons. Copper had many advantages over stone. It could be
melted and then molded into swords, battle-axes,
shields, helmets, and body armor. It was also more
reliable. A stone dagger might shatter in a fight, but
a copper weapon would probably remain whole.

The use of metal tools and weapons in place of
stone marks the end of the New Stone Age. But because stone tools were cheap and easy to make people continued to use them long after the introduction
of copper. Copper was very expensive. It usually
came from a far-off mountain or desert region. Very
few villages had copper mines outside their gate. It
was also difficult to work. Any farmer could chip out
a serviceable stone axe, but only a highly trained
smith who had devoted years to learning his craft
could make a good copper weapon. The cost therefore had to cover the services of the trader who
brought the copper from a distant mine and the
metal smith who turned it into a sturdy lance or
helmet.

Despite its cost the Mesopotamian villages had to

have copper because as they grew larger they began to fight with their neighbors over water rights and trade. Armed with stone they stood little chance of defeating enemies armed with copper and protected by copper shields and helmets. Whether they liked it or not they had to turn over a good part of their farm produce to the miner, trader, caravan driver, and smith. Though they now had the help of oxen and plows they found themselves working harder than ever before. And they had no choice. It was either *live with copper* or *perish without it.*

To protect themselves against enemy attack the villagers built high walls around their settlements. Some gave up farming altogether and joined a public works brigade that repaired dikes and canals and built fortifications. Others became merchants, priests, craftsmen, and officials.

As far back as fifty-five hundred years ago all the elements that make up a city began to fit into place in some of the Mesopotamian villages.

The villages were located where there was enough food and water for large numbers of people to live together in one confined place. The invention of the wheeled wagon and the sailing vessel allowed the villages to trade with distant places for necessary goods, such as copper. The use of the plow and irrigation supplied so much food that some people could give up farming altogether and live and work within the walls of the growing villages. Having been trained to work together on irrigation projects, people were able to turn to building roads, streets, government buildings, and temples. They were also able to accept the strong leadership necessary to run their giant communities.

As these villages along the Tigris and Euphrates grew in size and extended their rule over the surrounding countryside, the largest and most powerful of them became the first cities of mankind.

Soon after the cities of Mesopotamia arose, metalsmiths discovered that by adding a small amount of tin to copper they created bronze—a metal tougher and easier to work than copper. The Bronze Age began with the coming of the first cities.

The early farmer changed the environment by turning the wilderness into meadows, pastures, and farms. Yet he did not destroy the countryside. The builder of the first cities, however, erased the natural landscape, enveloped himself within high walls, and created a new man-made environment. *A model of a street in the city of Ur in Mesopotamia about four thousand years ago. In the background are the walls of the citadel and within, the temple tower of the chief god.*

THE RISE OF CIVILIZATION
Strangers, Dreamers, and Travelers

Chapter 7 Five thousand years ago most of the earth was still unchanged by the hand of man. Though there were farming villages scattered over the continents, the planet largely remained a great wilderness, the home of wild animals and small bands of wandering hunters. Only in the Middle East had man begun to make great changes in his physical surroundings.

Here he reshaped the landscape and built the first cities of the world.

The Bronze Age cities that rose along the banks of the Tigris and Euphrates rivers quickly became the masters of Mesopotamia. With their metal weapons and superior manpower they overran the remaining Stone Age villages and then proceeded to fight among themselves for land and trade. No city ruled more than twenty miles of the neighboring countryside. Yet each one was a proud independent nation with its own king, army, religion, and laws.

Men remodeled the landscape when they became city dwellers. In Mesopotamia they erected great walls, enormous palaces, and towering temples. In Egypt they built the pyramids, which were gigantic tombs for their dead kings. *The Great Pyramid of Cheops in Egypt—on the far right in this picture—is the largest ever built. A solid mass of limestone blocks, 768 feet square and 482 feet high, it is one of the Seven Wonders of the Ancient World.*

THE WORLD'S FIRST CITIES

Fifty-five hundred years ago the world's first cities arose in the Middle East along the Tigris and Euphrates rivers in Mesopotamia. Caravan drivers, sailors, and traders carried news about the new communities to remote areas. Within a few thousand years cities were created in other lands in Africa, Asia, and Europe. In America the Indians, knowing nothing about the Old World, built great cities of their own.

The map shows the approximate time cities arose in various parts of the world.

Pacific Ocean

Atlantic

MEXICO
1,500 years ago

CENTRAL AMERICA
1,800 years ago

PERU
2,500 years ago

Within their little cities people lived in a new man-made environment. Brick and stone replaced the trees and grass of the village. The air was crowded with the din of traffic, and the earth was scarred with muddied streets and cobbled squares. The sun seemed to vanish from the sky and hide in the shadow of crooked alleys.

Where a man lived depended on his rank and wealth. Within the center of the city was the closely guarded citadel, or fortress. Here, alongside the palace of the king and the temple of the chief god, dwelled the nobility and the priests. Outside the citadel the poor huddled in the world's first slums, housed in mud huts along narrow unpaved alleys

CHINA
3,500 years ago

CRETE
3,500 years ago

PAKISTAN
4,500 years ago

Pacific Ocean

EGYPT
5,000 years ago

MESOPOTAMIA
5,500 years ago

heaped with garbage. In the Mesopotamian city of Ur, the refuse was piled so high that the level of the streets gradually rose and householders were forced to build new entrances into the second story of their homes.

To a man who came from a little village the city was a strange and lonely place. In his village he had been surrounded by relatives who gave him understanding and shared what they had with him. But in the city he called few men by the sacred name of kin and brother. Outside his door there was no one on whom he could rely, no one to whom he could turn for help. He could go hungry while the sound of feasting and revelry rose from the other side of his neighbor's wall. The city was a gathering place of strangers.

Cut off from his kinsmen and suspicious of his neighbors, the new city dweller stopped caring about others. In the marketplace he bargained and cheated. In the shop in which he worked he took no pride in his labor.

Once he had been an all-round craftsman equally capable of shaping a stone tool, building a boat, or making a beautiful container. Now he was pinned down to one task, such as leather tanning or brick making. Day after day he followed the same dreary routine, and at his death his sons caught up his tools and continued where he left off.

In his village he had been his own master and set his own hours of work with time for games, ceremonies, and dancing. Now he worked from dawn until late at night in a factory attached to the palace of the king or to the temple of the chief god. In addition he could expect to be called upon at any time to repair city walls, dig irrigation ditches, or go off to fight in the endless wars against neighboring cities.

The farmer who cultivated the rich irrigated soil outside the city gates did not own his land but worked for the rulers of the city. He was a tenant of the king or chief priest who lent him land, farm tools, plows, oxen, and seeds and charged him enormous rates of interest. After the farmer had paid off his

In the Bronze Age cities the workers ate the same food, lived in the same dreary shelters, and labored all their lives at the same tasks. They were more slaves than free men. *Wall painting of workers making bricks for a noble's tomb in Egypt about thirty-five hundred years ago.*

debts and taxes, there was very little left for him and his family.

Both the city workers and the farmers were controlled and managed by their rulers almost as though they were animals attached to a plow or cart. The Stone Age society in which all men were equal had become a cruel dictatorship run for the benefit of kings, nobles, priests, and officials. People lost their freedom after they lost their rights to the land and its resources were gone.

Why did the people of the cities accept such an unfair arrangement?

Revolt was impossible. Armed warriors stood guard at the citadel gates. Jailers and executioners kept order. The king's guards, equipped with the latest metal weapons of war, were trained to crush civilian uprisings. And even if the rebels succeeded in defeating the soldiers, they would still have to storm the high walls of the citadel behind which the food reserves of the city were stored. They would starve long before the citadel fell.

Moreover, the king was guarded not only by the metal armor of his troops and the high walls of the citadel but by the gods themselves. In the early villages the farmers had believed that the gods were on their side and gave them plentiful harvests, good health, and large families. But when the early villages were conquered religious beliefs changed. People now believed that the gods had willed that they should suffer and that their rulers should prosper. Just as they were cut off from the land so, they believed, were they cut off from heaven and its blessings.

The chief god of the city was supposed to be the owner of the land and the factories. In his name the priests rented the fields to the farmers and supervised the work of the laborers and craftsmen in the

When the first cities of mankind arose in Mesopotamia and Egypt, the Stone Age villagers lost their freedom and became the subjects of powerful kings. In Mesopotamia the rulers frequently became both king and chief priest of the gods. In Egypt the pharaohs or kings were also worshiped as gods. *In 1965 when Egypt built the Aswan Dam on the upper reaches of the Nile River these great monuments were cut from the rock and removed to higher ground to save them from the rising waters of the dam.*

factories. Within the temple of the god, hundreds of servants kept busy preparing his food. But since the god never made an appearance at mealtime, the priests obligingly sat down and ate his food for him.

The actual owner of the land and factories was the king himself. In Mesopotamia he sometimes took two titles and was both king and high priest of the chief god. In Egypt he went one step further and insisted he was a god also.

Some kings, on the other hand, modestly claimed that they were only the servant or superintendent of the high god. While a king slept, the god appeared before him and gave him directions to build a new palace or monument or to declare war against a neighboring city. The god never seems to have asked for anything the king did not want for himself.

Why did the Mesopotamian rulers engage in such hocus-pocus?

By pretending that they were only carrying out the wishes of the god and not their own, the rulers increased their control over their people. For what man would dare to say *no* when the gods themselves had ordered him to toil all his life without reward or go off to die in a foreign war? The religion of the new cities taught people to accept a bitter fact: the vast wealth that came from the land and the factories was not intended for their benefit but for the benefit of their rulers.

Environmental warfare is the deliberate destruction of the land and its resources in order to defeat an enemy. It began when the first cities of Mesopotamia wrecked the irrigation systems of their rivals and it has continued to the present day. In the seventh century before Christ, King Sennacherib of Assyria boasted of his destruction of Babylon, the principal city of Mesopotamia: "The city and its houses I destroyed, I devastated, I burned with fire. The wall and the outer wall, temples, gods, and temple towers of brick and earth I razed . . . I flooded its site with water and the very foundations I destroyed. I made its destruction more complete than that by flood." *Mesopotamian warriors in battle.*

The wars among the rulers of the Bronze Age cities were almost continuous. The conflicts of the Ice Age hunters and the early farmers had been short-lived feuds rather than wars. But the conflicts of the Mesopotamian cities were fierce total struggles resulting in the destruction of armies and the massacre of thousands of men, women, and children.

Conquerors put houses to the torch, tore down city walls, and destroyed irrigation systems so that fields turned brown, crops withered, and animals died of thirst. Man waged war against the environment as well as against his fellow man.

An irrigation system should be able to last as long as the river that feeds it. In China people have been growing crops on irrigated soil for over four thousand years. Irrigation, however, requires constant care and work. When the farmers of Mesopotamia went off to fight their neighbors, dikes, reservoirs, and canals began to break down. In time, the neglect of the waterways as well as their deliberate destruction by enemy armies brought about the collapse of the entire irrigation system of Mesopotamia.

Today the proud cities of the Tigris and Euphrates are long vanished, together with the ancient waterways that brought them such vast wealth. Once a land of gardens, green meadows, and flowering orchards, much of Mesopotamia today is a parched desert under whose burning sands lie the ruins of lofty temples, vast palaces, and the statues of haughty kings who spoke to the gods in their dreams.

Men who turned the desert to fertile plain
Turned the land to desert again.

The early cities of mankind seem to have brought little benefit to most people. A semi-slave for priests and kings, the common man built fortifications, temples, and pyramids, piling up treasures he never enjoyed, and died unknown and unsung in a muddy alley, ignored by his neighbors, his rulers, and his gods. While he lived we may imagine him longing for the days when his forefathers lived at peace in tiny villages, worked for themselves, and enjoyed the companionship and protection of their kinsmen and neighbors.

Yet the early city, despite its many evils, brought man one overwhelming advantage. It brought him civilization.

Civilization means city living. It means such things as law, widespread trade, government, taxes, and police. It means science and writing.

Civilization also means that man became something different from what he was before.

Before man became civilized, that is before he became a city man, he had known only people who thought and behaved as he did, people like himself. They were the only people who mattered, the only people whom he considered real human beings. What happened inside his village was of more importance to him than anything else in the world. He could spend an entire lifetime without going beyond his village. He might hear the crowing of cocks and the barking of dogs from a nearby settlement and never visit it. Quick to come to the help of a fellow villager, he could look with indifference on the suffering of a stranger. His world ended at his village gate.

But once he came to live in the city, he became aware of the many differences among men. He began to realize that he was more than a member of a family, a band, or a tiny village. He was a part of a larger community of people from different places and with different ways of thinking and feeling.

The city also made him aware of the spaciousness of the world; it gave him a sense of geography. Located on a busy river or at a caravan crossroad, the city buzzed with news of far-off places. In the crowded marketplace, porters, caravan drivers, sailors, and traders filled the air with a babble of tongues. Not all men spoke the same language. At the city gate travelers appeared who might be

A master craftsman, a prophet, or a healer
A minstrel, builder, or storyteller.

Sensitive to new ideas and discoveries the city was a communications center. When a new method of metal working, textile making, or pottery appeared in one city, it spread rapidly to others. Soon after the first sail was invented, hundreds of sailing vessels were navigating the waters of the Tigris and Euphrates and then venturing out into the Persian Gulf and the Indian Ocean. The crafts of Mesopotamia were sold in the markets of India.

Traders and travelers carried word of the city way of life to the far corners of the Old World. The found-

The city is an environment made by man. Where the city rises the landscape is changed beyond recognition. Forests are cut down, rivers diverted, hills leveled, and the once green earth overlaid with asphalt and bristling towers. Neither storm, flood, nor earthquake can alter the face of nature more than a city. *Piccadilly Circus in central London.*

ing of one city led to the building of others, so that the early city, like the early farming village, spread far from its birthplace in the Middle East. Two thousand years after the first cities arose on the banks of the Tigris and Euphrates, people were living in cities in lands as far apart as Egypt, Crete, India, and China.

On the other side of the Atlantic Ocean, the American Indians received no word of the birth of cities in the Old World. Yet they built magnificent cities of their own in Mexico, Central America, and South America.

Civilization made people aware that there was a world beyond their village and beyond their city. It was an environment far larger and far richer than any they had imagined in the past. It was an environment filled with different ways of living. Not everyone thought as they did. Not everyone behaved as they did.

The city and its environment expanded man's idea of what it was to be a human being. In that way it made him different from what he was before.

Since the beginning of the Industrial Revolution two hundred years ago, huge machines have replaced the simple hand tools of the past. *At the controls of this powerful combine on a Canadian farm one man can harvest more wheat than a hundred men once did using sickles or scythes.*

MAN ALTERS THE ENVIRONMENT

Smog, Sewage, and Tar on Your Feet

During the long ages that man was a hunter and **Chapter 8** gatherer, he had little effect on the natural environment. Only after he became a farmer did he begin to change the land and its resources. He moved wild plants and animals out of the wilderness and transformed them into domestic crops and herds. As a potter reshapes clay, he reshaped the landscape, turning deserts into green fields and meadows.

73

Not content to use the resources of the earth in their natural form, he changed them to suit his purposes. He took the hard copper out of the ground and melted and molded it into tools, weapons, and household objects. Later, adding a little tin to the copper, he made bronze. A metal that had never existed in the earth, it was tougher than copper and also easier to work. Like nature itself, man became a creator of metals.

The greatest change man made in the environment came when he invented the city. Within its high walls he abolished the wilderness and in its place constructed a new landscape of streets, squares, markets, homes, palaces, and temples.

Still the ancient city builders generally did little widespread harm to the environment outside their walls. Beyond the boundaries of their little cities, the land was green, the air was clean, and the water fit to drink. It is true that the soldiers of Mesopotamia destroyed the fertile plains of "The Land Between the Rivers." But in other Bronze Age countries such as Egypt and China, land recovered from the desert by irrigation remained green for thousands of years.

OLD STONE AGE	NEW STONE AGE
大 大	大 大 大 大 大

Beginning of Farming	Beginning of C
10,000 years ago	*5,000 years a*

LONELY WILDERNESS TO OVERCROWDED PLANET

While man was a hunter and gatherer there were only about five million people on earth. A hunter could wander for a long time without meeting other human beings. With the birth of farming, however, the number of people on earth started to increase rapidly. Then with the Industrial Age about two hundred years ago, the population explosion was set off. By the beginning of the twentieth century, the human population exceeded the billion mark. Today it stands at three and one-half billion and by the end of the century it may reach seven billion.

Humans were once scarce creatures. Today they are among the most plentiful on the planet.

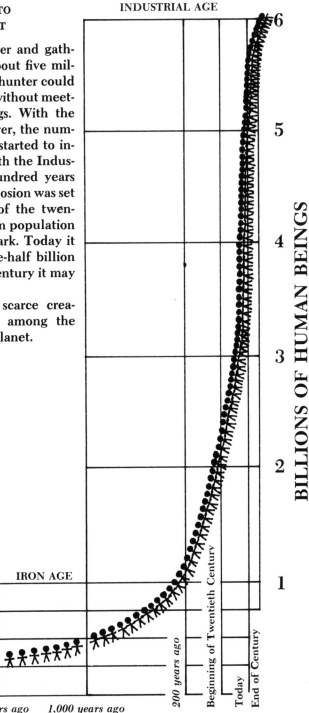

INDUSTRIAL AGE

BILLIONS OF HUMAN BEINGS

6

5

4

3

2

1

BRONZE AGE   IRON AGE

200 years ago

Beginning of Twentieth Century

Today

End of Century

2,000 years ago   1,000 years ago

It is only in our own time that man has begun to do widespread damage to the environment that gives him life.

Two hundred years ago, about the time that America became a free nation, there began a great change in human affairs that we call the Industrial Revolution. Beginning with the invention of the steam en-

Throughout the world, the automobile has brought about great changes in the land. An environmental failure, it loads the air with smog and covers vast sections of the countryside with asphalt and concrete. As traffic increases, more roads are built. Woods and meadows are destroyed to make way for motels, refreshment stands, shopping centers, gas stations, and car dumps. Although it was intended to speed the traveler along safely and quickly, the automobile has, in the great cities, actually slowed travel down. One hundred years ago a horse-drawn carriage could get through many of our cities faster than a car can today. *(below) The automobile has replaced the countryside with its own special scenery as in this photograph of Las Vegas, Nevada.*

Even when the automobile dies, it continues to injure the environment. *An automobile graveyard covers the side of a mountain in Vermont.*

gine, huge machines took the place of the simple hand tools of the past. The locomotive and later the automobile and the airplane took the place of animal transportation. Cities blazed with the light of artificial suns. Products unknown in nature poured out of the chemist's laboratory, such as synthetic fabrics, artificial rubber, medicines, pesticides, and fertilizers.

These inventions brought us comforts and luxuries undreamed of in the past. At the same time they had unforeseen effects on the environment. The simple tools of our ancestors, such as the hand hoe and the plow, were managed with human and animal labor and could not do much harm to the environment. But the mighty engines and generators of our industrial age are powered by the energy of coal, oil, and the atom, and create tremendous problems of pollution by giving off dangerous waste products.

Nowhere are the changes in the environment more noticeable than in the modern city.

We know that as the city grows and new buildings rise, the skyline changes. We may be unaware that the weather also changes. Yet if you listen to the weather report on a hot summer's day you know that the temperature in the city is higher than in the surrounding countryside.

Thousands of air conditioners pour waste heat into the streets, while at the same time the high buildings of the city block off cooling breezes. Then again, brick and stone, unlike grass, do not absorb the heat of the sun but bounce it back into the sweltering streets. It is also true that there is usually more rain in the city than in the countryside because the dust in the air triggers the condensation of moisture. A modern city makes its own climate.

It also makes its own noise. Ancient hunters and farmers lived in a deep stillness broken only by such natural sounds as the cry of wild animals or the rush of water over rocks and pebbles. We who live in the modern city are exposed to the roar of trains, the screeching of buses, the whine of refuse trucks, and the sonic boom of jets flying overhead. Within our homes, the racket made by the vacuum cleaner, the washing machine, the blender, and the electric hair dryer rivals the noise in the street. Modern man has created the noisiest environment of all time.

An industrial city has a special atmosphere of its own, called smog. Produced by a combination of automobile fumes and smoke, it hangs over many of the great cities of the world like an immovable cloud. In high concentrations it becomes a dangerous poison that kills trees, plants, animals, and people. Some years ago the city of London was blanketed for several days in a thick pea-soup haze that killed four thousand people.

In Los Angeles a citizen can tune in on a smog alert that announces when the air is not safe. But since he cannot stop breathing all he can do is stay indoors, watch the nearby mountains disappearing behind a mantle of brown mist, and listen to the sound of the poisoned fruit as it plops to the ground in his garden.

Modern industry has changed not only the air we breathe but the water we drink. Today we can buy thousands of new articles, ranging from color TV to plastic paints, that make life easier and pleasanter for us. Unfortunately, their production creates enormous quantities of waste materials. To dispose of

An industrial city creates an atmosphere of its own, called smog. Produced by a combination of smoke and automobile exhaust it blankets great cities such as Los Angeles, Tokyo, Rio de Janeiro, Mexico City, and New York. *Smog hanging over the city of New York as seen from the Empire State Building.*

these wastes manufacturers often dump them into the nearest stream or lake.

At the same time cities and villages throughout America pour millions of gallons of sewage into the waterways. Today there is not a single major river system in our country which is unpolluted. You can understand why people say, "Water just doesn't taste the way it used to."

Some of the new chemicals that farmers are using to increase the size of their crops are as dangerous to our waterways as industrial wastes or sewage. In the past farmers used the manure of their domestic animals to fertilize their fields. The modern farmer uses liquid nitrogen, a powerful artificial fertilizer that raises the yield of wheat and corn tremendously.

Unlike manure, however, not all the nitrogen is taken up by the soil. It has to go somewhere and that somewhere turns out to be a nearby river or lake. Here the nitrogen fertilizes algae and other water weeds and causes them to grow at an explosive rate. Worse still, some of the nitrogen sinks to the bottom of the water and becomes a dangerous poison. The farmer has increased the size of his crop and at the same time decreased the quality of the water he and his neighbors drink.

Pollution can actually kill a large body of water. Lake Erie, one of the five Great Lakes, is a huge freshwater inland sea. Until just a few years ago it provided pure drinking water, swimming, boating, and fishing for the people who lived along its banks. Every year fishermen took fifty million pounds of sturgeon, pike, and whitefish out of its clear waters. Today the catch is down to less than one thousand pounds.

What has happened is that the runoff of nitrogen from farmers' fields plus the sewage from the rapidly growing cities of the region have over-fertilized the lake. Weeds now cover large sections of the lake. As

Today man is polluting waterways all around the world. *One of the most beautiful waterways in the world, the Bay of Naples is rapidly becoming one of the most filthy.*

fast as the weeds grow they decay, using up the oxygen in the water so that the fish choke to death.

Wide areas of the lake are thick with muck and tar because chemical plants and oil refineries along the shore dump their wastes into the water. Recently one of the rivers flowing into the lake burst into flame fueled by oil leakage from one of the refineries. Lake Erie has become an open sewer.

What about the future? As the pollution increases and the weeds continue to spread over the surface, the lake will turn into a filthy marshland and finally dry up and disappear. Lake Erie has existed since the

Ice Age. Yet it has taken only a few short years for modern man to condemn it to death.

We know that people have been messy for a long time. Two thousand years ago the citizens of ancient Rome were complaining about bad air just as we do now. Six hundred years ago King Edward I of England ordered a householder put to the torture because the smoke of his coal fire annoyed his neighbors. In the past, however, pollution was usually limited to a small area. Today our ability to pollute the environment has become worldwide.

Winding its way through the city of Denver, the South Platte River is fouled with oil discharge, industrial wastes, and refuse.

Smoke pouring out of hundreds of factories in Western Germany is carried by the prevailing winds all the way to Norway and Sweden, where it falls as black snow. Mercury dumped into the sea by a chemical plant in Japan is eaten by swordfish which carry the poison across the wide Pacific to America. Oil tankers off the coast of North Africa empty their wastes into the Atlantic Ocean, and bathers from Cape Cod to Florida come home with tar on their feet. Hundreds of thousands of square miles of the Atlantic are now contaminated with garbage, sewage, and industrial wastes from countries on both sides of the ocean. A recent scientific expedition no-

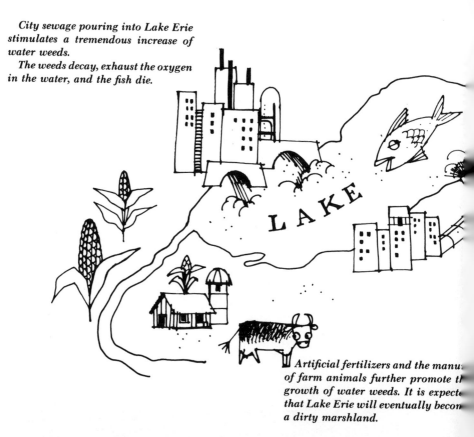

City sewage pouring into Lake Erie stimulates a tremendous increase of water weeds.

The weeds decay, exhaust the oxygen in the water, and the fish die.

Artificial fertilizers and the manu⸱ of farm animals further promote tⱨ growth of water weeds. It is expect⸱ that Lake Erie will eventually becom a dirty marshland.

ticed that vast sections of the Atlantic Ocean were covered with floating oil. In some places off the American coast and the Bahamas, the oil was so thick that it squeezed like spaghetti through the nets of the scientists.

When Thor Heyerdahl sailed his reed boat from Egypt to America he discovered huge patches of oil, filth, and plastic containers in the middle of the Atlantic. One thousand miles from land the water was so dirty that his crew could not take a dip. The refuse

Industrial plants dump oil wastes and other dangerous chemicals into the lake, shutting off light, killing water life, and destroying recreational and fishing facilities.

LAKE ERIE IS A DYING LAKE

In many industrial countries, rivers and lakes are being destroyed by pesticides, detergents, factory wastes, artificial fertilizers, and sewage.

Not even the great oceans are vast enough to handle all the wastes modern man dumps into them.

Today the rubbish of cities and industry litters the middle of the Atlantic Ocean. Oil wastes pumped overboard by oil tankers off the coast of North Africa float across the Atlantic and smear with tar beaches all the way from Maine to the islands of the Caribbean Sea.

Powerful pesticides such as DDT washed off farms into rivers and then into the ocean travel halfway around the world. Some of the pesticides have been found in birds and fish in lands as far away as Antarctica.

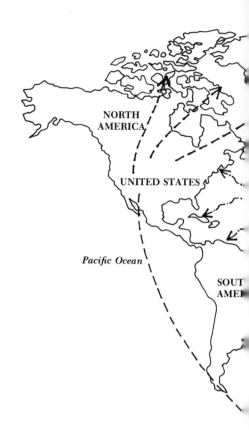

that raised the streets of ancient Ur has spread around the world.

No form of pollution travels farther than radioactive fallout. A waste product of nuclear bomb testing and the manufacture of nuclear power, radioactive fallout is carried by air currents high above the earth to the far corners of the planet. Rain and snow draw it to the ground where it is absorbed by plants. Animals eat the plants, and people eat the animals, so that children throughout the world are growing up with radioactive poisons in their bones.

Recently scientists were surprised to discover that

~.~.~-~-~· OIL WASTES

— — — — — — — PESTICIDES

Eskimos living in the Far North had a far greater concentration of radioactivity in their bodies than do people in the United States who live close to atomic power stations. The main food of these Eskimos is the caribou, or North American reindeer, an animal that lives on the lichen plant of the Arctic. Because the lichen cannot sink its roots into the frozen ground, it takes most of its nourishment from the atmosphere, which is contaminated with radioactive fallout.

The poison goes up the food chain. Concentrated in the tissues of the plant, it passes on to the caribou

Radioactive fallout from nuclear testing sites and atomic power plants is carried by wind currents to distant parts of the earth. Some of these wastes travel to the Far North, where they are absorbed by Arctic plants which are eaten by caribou (reindeer).

As the wastes are transferred from the plants to the animals they become concentrated. In this way, Eskimos who live on caribou meat are poisoned by fallout that comes from a source thousands of miles away.

Radioactive fallout, which is a waste product of nuclear bomb testing and the manufacture of nuclear energy for electrical power, is carried by air currents to many parts of the world. Although they live far off in the frozen north, Eskimo children today are carrying dangerous quantities of radioactive poisons in their bodies. *An Eskimo girl in Deering, Alaska, with her two small brothers.*

that graze on the lichen and finally to the Eskimos who live on the caribou. In this strange way the air we pollute at home gnaws at the bones of strangers in distant lands.

The environment is a communications network in

which everything in the world is connected with everything else. Man injured the environment in the past, but the harm he did was confined to his neighborhood, his city, or his country. Today the pollution created by our industrial age is planetary. Unhindered by national and natural boundaries and carried by ocean currents or winds high above the earth, it penetrates into the farthest corners of the globe. Let one nation test a nuclear bomb and the message of death is blown around the earth.

Not the gardens of Mesopotamia but all the lands of the earth are now in danger.

Of all the planets, only the earth provides a suitable environment for man. In the last two hundred years, however, man has done serious injury to the planet and the time may come when his only home in space will be hurt beyond all healing. *Astronaut John Young's view of the earth from the Command Module when it was approximately 100,000 miles away in June 1969.*

A PLANET IN DANGER
The Great Whales and Plastic Bottles

Seen from the depths of space, the earth is a beautiful **Chapter 9** blue and white island floating gracefully in the sky among its sister planets. Yet it is, in some ways, quite different from the other planets that circle the sun. It is enclosed in a protective layer of air, blanketed in green vegetation, and wet with oceans, streams, and lakes. Alone among the planets of the solar system, and perhaps among all the planets of the uni-

Throughout the world fish and waterbirds are being killed off because of the pollution of rivers, lakes, and seas. *Morrison Creek is a pleasant little stream that wanders through Sacramento County, California, until it reaches the Sacramento River. In 1970 pollution from a mysterious source destroyed a thousand carp and sunfish along with frogs and other water life.*

verse, the earth provides a perfect environment for higher forms of life, including man.

Today, that life-giving environment is under serious attack by man himself.

Among the principal resources of the environment are the wild animals of the earth. The early farmers as well as the ancient hunters preyed on the animals for food but made no effort to wipe them out. In the last two hundred years, however, modern man has deliberately exterminated species on which his ancestors lived for thousands of years.

When the white man came to America, sixty million buffalo ranged the prairies. Within a one-hundred-year period, almost all of them were killed off by the guns of frontiersmen and soldiers. At the present time, except for the scraggly creatures in city zoos and a few small tame herds, the buffalo are gone from America.

In 1806 a traveler in Kentucky sighted a flock of passenger pigeons that measured over a mile wide and 240 miles long. After a century of senseless slaughter this most numerous of American birds has

Waterbirds quickly fall victim to oil discharges, industrial wastes, and poisons such as DDT that find their way into waterways. *A badly polluted area on the Gulf Coast of Texas, south of Houston.*

been completely wiped out. Other animals that may soon meet the fate of the passenger pigeon include the timber wolf, the grizzly bear, and the bald eagle, the proud emblem of our country.

The coldest and deepest regions of the ocean cannot protect the animals from man's unending pursuit. The great whales, the largest creatures that ever lived on earth, are in danger of extinction. Despite their size and power they have no chance against modern whaling vessels equipped with radar, sonar, scout planes, electrically controlled guns, and other instruments of modern warfare. We treat the whales as though they were our mortal enemy and not one of our precious natural resources.

As we exhaust the wildlife of the planet, so we exhaust metals, coal, oil, and other vital resources. Since the day a farmer in the Middle East shaped a piece of copper into a bit of jewelry for his wife, man has been making use of the treasures hidden beneath the surface of the earth. Today we are recklessly consuming these resources at a faster and faster rate, forgetting that they are not replaceable. Projects such as voyages to the moon take up enormous quantities of metals and natural fuels. Unless we learn to conserve our resources the time is not far distant when no matter how deep we dig there will be no copper, iron, tin, coal, oil, or natural gas left anywhere on earth.

Much of the coal in America is found just a few feet beneath the earth and is brought to the surface by gigantic strip-mining machines. As these man-made monsters dig into the earth, they choke meadows with rocks, choke streams with debris, and cut down forests, hills, houses, and even graveyards. They have scarred millions of acres of the American countryside. *A hillside in Schuylkill County, Pennsylvania, after a strip-mining machine passed through in 1959.*

Can we exhaust the air about us?

Every engine now running in the world, whether in a factory, automobile, train, or airplane, consumes air. A jet liner gulps down thirty-five tons of oxygen every time it crosses the Atlantic. As we build more engines, we dip further and further into our planet's store of air.

It is true that the forests of the earth are continuously producing oxygen. But it is also true that we are cutting down the forests. Today Brazil plans to level

most of its enormous Amazonian rain forest to make way for farms, ranches, highways, and new cities. It has been estimated that the destruction of so much green vegetation would deprive the planet of one-fifth of its supply of oxygen. In which case, we might all be left gasping for breath. /

Not only do our modern machines injure the environment, but so do many of the products turned out by those machines. Until just a few years ago our clothing was made of wool, cotton, and silk. Our tires were made of natural rubber. Our cleaners were made of soap and our bottles of glass. All of these were natural products which eventually broke up, decayed, and disappeared into the earth. Nature takes care of its own wastes.

But in the last twenty-five years we have learned to manufacture materials that never existed in nature. Among these are plastics, detergents, pesticides, and synthetic fabrics such as dacron and nylon. Substances created by man in the laboratory cannot easily break down and decay.

A clay pot or a glass bottle crumbles and becomes a part of the soil from which it originally came. But the material of a plastic bottle will remain to haunt our great-great-grandchildren. Even the great ocean cannot dissolve it. That is why we are seeing so much plastic on the beaches nowadays.

Man has used soap for thousands of years without harm to himself or the environment. The detergents

One of our most valuable planetary resources is the top soil on which we grow our food. Yet because of the cutting down of forests and overgrazing by cattle, tremendous amounts are lost each year. Rain water, no longer held by the roots of grasses and trees, runs off the land and carries the soil along with it. In many places the earth begins to look like the surface of the moon. *(left) A donkey searches for a few miserable blades of grass in an eroded field in Colombia, South America. (below) It is hard to believe that this California hillside was once green and covered with thick woods. But since men cut down the trees and allowed their cattle to eat all the grass, only where the lone oak tree digs its roots into the ground does any top soil still remain.*

that we now use in its place, however, have had some very surprising results. Like other synthetic products, these detergents don't break down. Poured into the kitchen drain, they find their way into wells and waterways and finally back into our drinking water. In some communities in America water from the faucet foams like beer from the tap.

DDT is a synthetic insect poison used in great quantities throughout the world. You may get rid of a can of DDT by tossing it into your refuse pail. But though the sanitation department takes it away, it really has not gone away. Thrown on a garbage dump, the DDT seeps into underground streams and then into rivers or the sea, where it may be consumed by fish and, finally, by the people that eat the fish. No matter where it goes DDT will continue to pollute the earth for many generations to come.

Half a million man-made chemicals are in use today. Yet we know little of their effect once they are released into the environment. We do know that DDT and other pesticides have already killed alarming numbers of birds and fish.

Ancient people were polluters. But they were short-term polluters. Whatever harm they did to the environment was limited in time. Their clothing and many of their tools decayed and disappeared, their houses and pottery returned to mud. Their metals

rusted and sank into the earth. Our nylons, pesticides, detergents, and plastics, on the other hand, are
not changed by the passage of the years. They travel
far and live long. That may be good for the archaeologists who someday may want to know what Industrial
Man was like, but it is bad for us. We have given
eternal life to junk.

We manufactured these new products because of
their obvious advantages. DDT kills insects that
breed disease. Plastic bottles don't break as glass bottles do. Synthetic rubber tires outlast natural rubber,
and dacron holds a crease far better than wool. We
certainly did not intend to harm the environment.

Sometimes, however, we *do* intend to harm the
environment.

Environmental warfare is the deliberate destruction of the natural environment in order to injure the
enemy in time of war. It began when the Bronze Age
warriors of Mesopotamia wrecked the irrigation systems of their rivals, and it has continued down to the
present day. In the nineteenth century in America
the soldiers and frontiersmen wiped out the buffalo
herds in order to starve the Indians to death. They
knew that the destruction of natural resources could
be far more deadly than one hundred pitched bat-
tles. It was not long before the whitened bones of the

Indians mingled with those of the buffalo on the prairies.

During the Vietnam war, magnificent rain forests and plantations were bombed until not a tree was left standing. Rice lands were sprayed with poisonous chemicals. Even the weather was tampered with by setting off cloud bursts to flood the countryside. Once one of the most beautiful and fertile lands on earth, large sections of Vietnam now resemble a barren moonscape.

We call our planet *the solid earth*. Yet this globe floating in space to which three and one-half billion

Life exists only on the earth's thin skin of water, soil, and air. The increased burning of coal and oil is filling the air with dangerous poisons and reducing the amount of oxygen in the atmosphere. The time may soon come when the air will be unable to contain all the gases and smoke now being poured into it. *Clouds of smoke from an industrial plant hang over a city in West Germany and hide the light of the sun.*

of us are clinging is unbelievably sensitive. Only the biosphere (the small portion made up of the water area, the land surface, and the air) is at all capable of supporting life.

If we continue, whether in peace or war, to abuse the environment, the air will be unable to contain all the smoke and gases pouring into it every day. The streams, lakes, and oceans will be unable to accept the industrial wastes and sewage. The junk will devour our living space.

Man's only home in the solar system will have become unfit for man.

We have always considered ourselves superior to the people who lived in the distant past. Did we not level mountains, raise skyscrapers into the clouds, and fling great bridges across wide waterways? We stamped out plagues that once killed millions and discovered new sources of energy within the atom. We snapped the gravitation chains that bound us to the earth and walked on the moon. Early man had been the slave of the environment, but modern man had become its master.

Today, however, when we drink a glass of water foaming with detergent, come home from the beach with tar on our feet, or watch the smog settling down over the rooftops, we begin to look less like the masters and more like the victims. We have changed the environment. We have also endangered our planet.

Ten thousand years ago man was one of the rarest creatures on the planet. Today we number three and one-half billion and by the year 2000 there may be seven billion of us. Should the population explosion continue at the present rate the globe will be as thickly inhabited two hundred years from now as the city of New York is today. *An aerial view of the bathing beach at Coney Island, New York.*

THE EARTH IS SACRED
Dolphins and People

Chapter 10 Fire Island is a thirty-four-mile-long ribbon of white sand in the Atlantic Ocean off the coast of New York. It is a landscape of unfenced beach and dune, groves of black pine and holly cut flat by the sea winds, and ground covers of wild rose and blackberry. Each fall, flocks of wild geese in V formation fly south along the shore line, long-legged heron stand guard in the salt marshes, and deer browse in the thickets along the bay.

For years I have walked along the curving shore,

collecting pebbles, shells, and curious pieces of glass worn smooth by the waves, and watched the sea gulls noisily circling overhead. Occasionally, a school of dolphins just beyond the line of breakers kept up with me on my walks as though to keep me company. I have sometimes imagined that time has stood still on Fire Island and that the beach, the sea, the animals, and the twisted trees are as they were in ancient times.

The other day, however, when I came home from my walk, my feet were sticky with blobs of tar, and I was reminded that Fire Island has not escaped the problems of our age. For weeks each summer the beach is covered with purple-black pools of tar and oil slick dumped from passing ships. Clusters of dead fish are washed up by the incoming tide. The sea gulls hunt for shellfish among plastic bottles, beer can packs, and nylon cording. I have not sighted the dolphins for several years now.

The landscape itself is changing. When I first came to Fire Island the sand dunes that guarded the beach against the pounding seas stood over twenty-five feet high. Today they have almost disappeared.

Home owners built their houses on the edge of the beach and loosened the dune sand. Then during the high tides of winter the sea flattened the weakened dunes. Some years ago the waves unhindered by any natural beach defenses swept over a section of the

Along the ocean front, dunes are natural defenses against the force of the waves. When man builds houses and roads close to the ocean he destroys the dunes and causes great damage to the shore. *The beach after a storm at Fire Island. Man changes the natural environment at his peril.*

island carrying houses, telephone poles, and even sidewalks from ocean to bay.

Great South Bay on the north side of the island has become increasingly polluted by the sewage from the towns on the mainland. Half the clam beds are contaminated and the famous Great South Bay oysters have almost disappeared.

Wastes from the duck farms along the shore add to the pollution in the bay and at the same time stimulate the growth of water weeds. Forming mats of vegetation thick enough to stand on, the weeds are swept up on Fire Island, where they decay and turn into an ill-smelling green slime. I no longer swim or fish in the Great South Bay.

The time may come when the Great South Bay will be transformed into a dirty marsh, and Fire Island ground into a hundred tiny sandbars. The fault will not be nature's but our own. For we are doing to this narrow ribbon of Atlantic beach what we have been doing to other parts of the earth since the beginning of the Industrial Age. We are making it unfit for human life.

The great scientific accomplishments of the last two hundred years tricked us into believing that we could do anything we pleased with the earth. There seemed to be no reason why we should not dump our sewage into the waterways, cut down the forests, or burn fuels that filled the sky with smoke and poisonous fumes.

If the environment was hurt that was not our concern because after all the environment was something outside ourselves, something apart from us. A river was not a human being, only a thing to be controlled and mastered for our benefit and convenience.

What we did not realize was that we humans are as much a part of the environment as the animals, the plants, the water, the air, and the soil. What we do to the environment we do to ourselves. Today we drive off the dolphins. Tomorrow it may be our turn to be driven off!

It is pretty certain that we cannot return to the days before civilization when people lived in small

It is hard to realize that the tremendous changes man has made on the land are very recent. One hundred years ago Herman Melville, the author of *Moby Dick*, was still able to say:

> "My eyes rolled over the wide rolling country
> and over the village and over a farmhouse
> here and there and over woods, groves, rocks
> and falls—and I thought to myself what a
> slight mark does man make over this huge green earth."

Today much of "this huge green earth" is covered with super-highways, parking lots, car dumps, factories, motels, and the ever swelling suburbs of great cities. Man's mark on the earth is no longer slight. *The American countryside as Melville may have seen it; farmland near York, Pennsylvania.*

communities and man's mark on the earth was light. A few young people may escape to communes in the country and lead a simple life close to the land. Most of us, however, will continue to live in our modern cities and towns and take advantage of the inventions and discoveries of our age.

Nevertheless, there are a number of things we can do to reduce the attack on the environment.

We can turn to natural products rather than to synthetics whether in the form of artificial rubber tires, pesticides, or clothing. It should not be hard to give up detergents for old-fashioned soap. We have to improve our power plants and machines to make them pollution-free. The thought of discharging dangerous automobile exhausts into the open air should be as horrible to us as discharging them into our living room.

To save our steadily decreasing store of natural resources from vanishing altogether, we have to reuse many of the articles we are now throwing away. The newspaper we recycle helps to preserve our forests. We must also be willing to take better

Man can be good to his environment. In the west, great dams have transformed deserts into rich farmland, created magnificent new lakes and reservoirs, and provided recreation for millions of people. *Grand Coulee Dam on the Columbia River, Washington. In the background you see a great body of water created by man: the 151-mile-long Franklin D. Roosevelt Lake, reaching all the way to the Canadian border.*

care of our equipment and make it last longer. We can learn to be proud of our "vintage" car or refrigerator.

We must be ready to give up programs such as space exploration that use enormous quantities of our diminishing fuels and metals. We succeed in landing three men on the moon on schedule but encounter all sorts of traffic problems when we try to get to school or work on time. Space travel can wait until we have taken care of travel on this planet.

Above all else, we have to learn to respect this fragile earth of ours.

Primitive people understand man's relationship to the environment better than we do. Far removed from civilization in distant jungles and remote deserts, they live today very much the way their hunting and farming ancestors did thousands of years ago. When they look upon a stream, a tree, or an animal, they see not a thing but a spirit or god. Though they may use it, they may never abuse it. For them a lake has as much right to exist as any human being.

Many of us, on the other hand, have another way of looking at nature. We see it as a bundle of things set down on earth for our convenience and comfort. We treat Lake Erie with as much respect as an old stove put out at the curb for the junkman to cart away.

One of the great triumphs of man in reshaping the earth has been the reclaiming of land from the sea. In Holland in ancient times the Dutch protected themselves against the rising tides by constructing large mounds on which they built their homes and grew their crops. Later they built dykes or sea walls. *In 1928 the land you see in the background was reclaimed from the water with the help of the powerful pumping station in the middle of the picture. Fields, roads, bridges, and villages are well below the surface of the sea on the other side of the dyke. Crops now grow and cattle graze where once fish swam.*

When we hunt, we hunt not for food but amusement. The slaughtered animal at our feet is only a trophy we can boast about to our friends. A primitive hunter, however, kills only when driven by necessity. So close is his feeling of kinship for the slain animal that he will frequently ask its forgiveness for what he has been forced to do.

Today we are in serious trouble—not only with the animals, but with all of nature. We have failed to see that though we may abuse the soil or water or air for a time, eventually we must pay a price. If we are to survive on this planet, we will have to give up struggling with the environment and learn to cherish our earth and its life-giving treasures.

Born on this earth more than one million years ago, man today stands at the peak of his power. The lowly, homeless creature who wandered through the wilderness uncertain of his food or his destination, a crude stone axe clutched in his hand, now controls the destiny of a planet. His vehicles travel the air faster than the speed of sound. His machines make mountains tremble and his footprints set up clouds of dust on the moon.

Unfortunately, however, as his power to improve his way of life has increased, so has his power to damage the earth. The automobile that brings him freedom of movement fills the air with pollution. The pesticides that enlarge his harvests poison his water. The oil that warms his home smudges the beaches of the world.

The power of man now rivals tornado, tidal wave, and earthquake. His strip mines uproot great forests, his nuclear tests submerge islands under the sea, and his industrial wastes destroy waterways. He has paid a high price for whatever benefits he has gained.

Towards the end of the last century, the English writer H.G.Wells wrote a science fiction story called "The War of the Worlds" in which creatures from Mars armed with fantastic weapons of destruction attack the earth. Wells did not dream that the real assault on our planet would be made—not by invaders from outer space—but by its own human inhabi-

Nothing about man says that he must abuse the environment. For many thousands of years he managed to live in harmony with nature just as he still does in remote parts of the world. Remembering how much they owe to nature, primitive people cherish the land and its resources. *A native hunter in Arnhem Land, Australia.*

tants. Today we are called upon to defend the earth from ourselves.

Yet we need not be our own enemy. Nothing about our history says that we must destroy the earth that has nourished us and given us the means to build civilization. Man once was kind to the environment; he can be kind again. Like the ancient farmers and hunters, we, too, can live in harmony with all of nature.

When we do, the rivers will run clean again. The air will be fit to breathe and the water to drink. The constellations will blaze as brightly in the night sky as they did ten thousand years ago, before man left the green and quiet wilderness.

Dictionary for the Environment

Agricultural Revolution: The change in man's way of life as he turned from hunting and gathering to farming.

Agriculture: The farming of broad fields using the plow. Before the invention of the plow, people were not agriculturists but gardeners. Agriculture has changed the environment of vast areas of the earth.

Algae: Plants including seaweeds living in fresh and salt water; some are microscopic, others are many feet long. It is the scum-forming, blue-green algae that kill off other forms of water life.

Anthropology: The study of man. Some anthropologists live among primitive people for a time in order to understand their way of life.

Archaeology: The study of ancient people by examining whatever is left of their cities, villages, monuments, and tools. The archaeologist digs into the earth to find the ruins of early settlements.

Biosphere: That small part of the planet that supports life, including the waterways and oceans, the surface of the earth, and the atmosphere close to it.

Bronze: A man-made metal, a mixture of copper with a little tin, that produces a tool or weapon which is tougher and sharper than one made only of copper.

Bronze Age: The time beginning first in the Middle East about five thousand years ago when people built the first cities and gradually gave up stone tools for those made of bronze.

Civilizations: Societies having cities, specialist workers, record keeping such as writing, science, and powerful governments. Civilizations arose with the first cities fifty-five hundred years ago.

DDT: A very powerful insect killer (dichlorodiphenyl trichloroethane). A man-made substance that does not break down into a harmless form, DDT accumulates in increasing amounts in the soil and water.

Detergents: Cleansing substances. Those that contain phosphates stimulate the growth of water weeds that consume the oxygen in lakes and streams and thereby destroy fish life.

Domestication: The turning of wild plants and animals into varieties that can be cared for and cultivated by man. The principal food crops of the world, including wheat, barley, corn, and rice, were once wild plants.

Ecology: Study of the relation between a plant or animal and its environment. The first part of the word *(eco)* comes from the Greek term meaning household. Ecology takes in the entire household of nature. Human ecology deals with the relation between human beings and the environment. Ecology is a two-way street: the environment influences people, and people in turn influence the environment.

Environment: Man's surroundings, including not only the place where he lives but the altitude, climate, rainfall, temperature, etc. It also includes what man himself has made, such as the city, tools, inventions, science, and art.

Environmental warfare: The deliberate destruction of an enemy's land and water resources, including even attempts to alter the weather.

Eutrophication: The aging of a lake until it gradually changes into a marsh and finally disappears. Man hastens the process by dumping sewage, animal wastes, and detergents and thereby setting off a massive growth of water weeds. As the weeds multiply, the lake slowly dries up.

Fallout: Radioactive wastes released into the atmosphere by the testing of nuclear bombs or by industrial plants producing nuclear energy that are carried by air currents and eventually come down to earth.

Fertilizers: Substances including human and animal manure and chemicals such as phosphates and liquid nitrogen that help the growth of plants but also harm the waterways. In many parts of the world, farmers depend on chemical fertilizers to raise their crops.

Forest folk: Hunting and gathering bands that lived in Europe about twelve thousand years ago as the Ice Age ended and our present climate began.

Gatherers: Primitive people (who also hunt) who collect wild plant food, honey, insects, and shellfish. Gathering is no simple matter of shaking a bush and allowing the berries to fall into a basket. The West Coast Indians, for example, who gathered acorns, knew the secret of getting rid of the tannic acid in the nuts to make them fit to use as food.

Industrial Revolution: The changes in living in Western countries beginning about two hundred years ago brought about by new inventions and technology, including the use of steam for power and the development of canals, roads, rail and steamboat travel, and factories.

Irrigation: The bringing of water to dry regions by means of dams, reservoirs, channels, and ditches.

Mayan Indians: Ancestors of the present-day Indians of Yucatan and southern Mexico who created a great civilization long before Columbus arrived in America.

Mesopotamia: Southern Iraq, the land watered by the Tigris and Euphrates rivers where the first cities of mankind arose.

Middle East: Region south and east of the Mediterranean Sea from Egypt in the west to Turkey, Iraq, and Iran in the east, where people first learned to farm and build cities.

Natufians: Southwest Asian hunting and gathering bands living at the eastern end of the Mediterranean Sea, among the first people to experiment with raising plants and animals.

Nature: The original or wild state of the environment that has not been fundamentally altered by man. The oceans, the mountains, the forests, and the wild animals are all part of nature. Along with butterflies, buffalo, and whales, man still depends on nature in order to live. Unlike the animals, however, man *can* interfere in the processes of nature as when he reshapes the environment about him.

Obsidian: A hard, black glass that comes out of the depths of volcanoes, used by New Stone Age farmers to make tools and weapons.

Pesticides: Powerful chemical poisons, such as DDT, for destroying insect pests. Unfortunately, pesticides kill not only harmful insects, but also birds, fish, and other useful animals.

Plow: Farming implement for turning over the soil, pulled by animals or powered by an engine.

Pollution: Fouling the environment as by sewage, industrial by-products, or animal wastes.

Pottery: Articles made of clay, such as pots, vases, and grain and water containers, invented by New Stone Age farming people.

Pueblo: A village of Indians, such as the Zuni, living in the southwestern United States.

Recycle: To change in such a way that the original condition is re-established. For example, newspaper can be recycled and then used again.

Sickle: A hand tool for cutting down grains and grasses. Its blade may be made of stone, bone, clay, or metal.

"Slash and burn": A way of farming in which crops are planted in forest clearings after the trees have been burned down. The ashes make an excellent, though temporary, fertilizer.

Smog (SMoke + fOG): Mixture of smoke and fog.

Specialist: New Stone Age workers who did no farm work but specialized in brickmaking, weaving, jewelry making, house-building, and other trades and occupations.

Synthetics: Substances created in the chemical laboratory such as DDT, nylon, or plastics as opposed to those of natural origin such as cotton or wood.

Tell: An artificial hill, the result of building settlements on the ruins of older ones. When you dig into a tell, you notice that it is arranged roughly like a layer cake. The ruins of the earliest community appear at the bottom and each succeeding level of settlement comes closer to the top.

For Further Reading

Caudill, Harry M. MY LAND IS DYING. New York: E. P. Dutton & Co., Inc., 1971. *What happens to people when farms and homes are destroyed by strip mining machines tearing away at the surface of the earth for coal. Magnificent photographs.*

Clark, Grahame. THE STONE AGE HUNTERS. New York: McGraw-Hill, Inc., 1971. (Also available in paperback.) *An account of man as he changes from Old Stone Age hunter to farmer. Illustrated with pictures of present-day Stone Age people.*

Harrison, C. William. CONSERVATION: THE CHALLENGE OF RECLAIMING OUR PLUNDERED LAND. New York: Julian Messner, 1963. *Very good photographic documentation on pollution; includes some material on worldwide aspects of the subject.*

Jennings, Gary. THE SHRINKING OUTDOORS. Philadelphia: J. B. Lippincott Company, 1973. *A comparison of the environment of earlier times to that of today with suggestions of ways to stop pollution.*

Mellaart, James. CATAL HÜYÜK: A NEOLITHIC TOWN IN ANATOLIA. New York: McGraw-Hill, Inc., 1967. *The story of the excavation of the huge farming community and trading center that flourished at the beginning of the New Stone Age. Remarkable illustrations.*

Mellaart, James. EARLIEST CIVILIZATIONS OF THE NEAR EAST. New York: McGraw-Hill, Inc., 1966. (Also available in paperback.) *The archaeologist who excavated Catal Hüyük relates the story of man in the Middle East from the days of the Ice Age to the rise of the first cities.*

Pfeiffer, John E. THE SEARCH FOR EARLY MAN. New York: American Heritage Publishing Co., Inc., 1963. *Beautifully illustrated story of man before the age of farming.*

Pringle, Laurence P. ONE EARTH, MANY PEOPLE: THE CHALLENGE OF HUMAN POPULATION GROWTH. New York: The Macmillan Company, 1971. *A clear, easy-to-read discussion of the effects of over-population on man and his environment.*

Sears, Paul B. LANDS BEYOND THE FOREST. New Jersey: Prentice-Hall, Inc., 1969. *An account of the inescapable relation between man and the land which he continues to depend upon today just as he did in the past.*

Shuttlesworth, Dorothy E. CLEAN AIR-SPARKLING WATER: THE FIGHT AGAINST POLLUTION. Garden City, New York: Doubleday & Company, Inc., 1968. *Very good photographic documentation on pollution with some reference to its worldwide aspects.*

Weisgard, Leonard. THE FIRST FARMERS IN THE NEW STONE AGE. New York: Coward, McCann & Geoghegan, Inc., 1966. *Clear explanation of life in the New Stone Age, based on archaeological studies. Stresses the influence of man's discovery of agriculture upon primitive society development.*

Woodwell, G. M., H. M. Malcolm and R. H. Whitaker. A-BOMBS, BUG BOMBS, AND US. Upton, New York: Brookhaven National Laboratory, 1966. *A lively explanation with clever cartoons of the dangers in pesticides and pollution from atomic fallout.*

Index

Africa, 12, 13, 19, 22, 39, 47, 60, 84, 86
Agricultural Revolution, 18–19, 26, 112
Agriculture, 54, 112
Algae, 81, 112
America. *See* United States
Animals: danger to, 92–94; of Ice Age, 2–3, 4, 5, 6, 7, 18; as source of power, 52–53, 54. *See also* Domestication of animals
Anthropology, 112
Archaeology, 15, 42, 99, 112
Arctic, 1, 5, 6, 87, 88
Asia, 2, 6, 12, 13, 80. *See also* Southwest Asia
Atlantic Ocean, 12, 61, 85, 86
Atmosphere, danger to, 79, 84, 86–90, 95–96, 101. *See also* Environment and air
Australia, 7, 9, 12, 16, 111
Automobile, 76, 77, 95, 107, 110

Bering Strait, 2, 6
Biosphere, 101, 112
Bow and arrow, 7, 8, 19. *See also* Weapons
Bronze, 57, 74, 112. *See also* Weapons
Bronze Age, 57, 59, 63, 67, 75, 112

Canada, 1, 5, 73
Caribou, 5, 12, 13, 26–28, 87–89. *See also* Eskimos
Catal Hüyük, 12, 13, 26, 27, 28, 43
Cavemen, 3–7, 8, 11; paintings of, 3, 4, 5, 8
Chieftains, 42

Cities, 14, 30, 40, 43, 59, 106, 112, 113; as communications centers, 70, 71; first, 48, 57, 58, 60, 68–69, 114; kings of, 52, 60, 62, 63, 64, 65, 66; in Mesopotamia, 48, 52, 56–57, 60–68; spread of, 60, 71; slums of, 60–61; workers in, 62–63
Civilization, 17, 34, 40, 69, 105, 112
Clay, 21, 22–23, 48, 73, 114. *See also* Pottery
Climate, 2–3, 4, 5, 6, 8, 38, 113
Clothing, 2, 3, 4, 5, 9, 41, 44, 106
Copper, 55–57, 74, 112. *See also* Weapons

Dams, 52, 107
DDT, 86, 93, 98–99, 112, 114, 115
Detergents, 85, 97–99, 101, 107 113
Domestication, of animals, 8, 11, 13, 14, 17–18, 31; of plants, 11, 13, 14, 15–17, 31

Earth, 2, 6, 18, 58, 75, 91, 92, 100, 108, 109, 110, 111, 113
Ecology, 113
Egypt, 10, 12, 33, 61, 65, 66, 71, 74, 86; pyramids of, 59
England, 2, 6, 37, 39, 84
English Channel, 2, 6
Environment, 21, 37, 38, 51, 77, 79, 84, 86–87, 88, 89, 90, 95–96, 100–01, 105, 108–09, 112; and air, 76, 79, 84, 86–87, 88, 89, 90, 95–96, 100–01; and the city, 58, 60, 69–74, 78–80; as a communications net-